Journeying with Jesus
a companion's guide

Denis McBride

By the same author

Borrowing the Eyes of Others: Reflecting with Paintings, Volume I
Awakening to Yourself: Reflecting with Paintings, Volume II
Where Does the Jesus Story Begin?
Waiting on God
Jesus and the Gospels
Seasons of the Word: Reflections on the Sunday Readings
The Parables of Jesus
Impressions of Jesus
The Gospel of Mark
The Gospel of Luke
Emmaus: the Gracious Visit of God

Where Does the Jesus Story Begin? – set of 10 lectures on CD
Jesus and the Gospels – set of 36 lectures on CD

Visit: www.denismcbride.com

For Melca,

across a world,
in respect and gratitude

Copyright © Redemptorist Publications, 2009

Published by **Redemptorist Publications**
A Registered Charity limited by guarantee. Registered in England 3261721.

First published February 2009

Layout and cover design by Chris Nutbeen
Front cover illustration from istockphoto

ISBN 978-0-85231-358-9

A CIP catalogue record for this book is available from the British Library

Printed by Cavendish, Leicester

Redemptorist
PUBLICATIONS

Alphonsus House Chawton Hampshire GU34 3HQ
Telephone 01420 88222   01420 88805
rp@rpbooks.co.uk   www.rpbooks.co.uk

The Journey

Before setting out

Dear Reader,

You are very welcome to these reflections on Jesus' journey. After being in Hawkstone Hall, the Redemptorist international pastoral centre in Shropshire, for twenty-one years, I was appointed publishing director of Redemptorist Publications. Soon after my arrival, the marketing manager, Trish Wilson, said to me: "Denis, I was thinking that we really do need an RP book for Lent, a companion guide that could be a real help to individuals but also to groups. And I was wondering…"

As the sentence trailed off into the Hampshire countryside it was replaced by a large hopeful smile. I smiled back, somewhat wearily, I have to confess, but took the cue. Do it, I said to myself. And then to Trish, I announced over-solemnly: "It will be done."

That conversation has resulted in this book, *Journeying with Jesus: A Companion's Guide*. Although the idea began as a Lenten companion, the book has enlarged itself into a series of reflections on the journey of Jesus, which can be used at any time of the year. These reflections have been edited by Andrew Lyon, the editorial manager of RP, to produce also a workbook aimed specifically for group use: *Journeying with Jesus: A Companion's Guide for Groups*.

For the books, I decided to choose seven places, out of many others, associated with Jesus in the Gospels and write about seven stations from the wilderness to the tomb, and beyond. These stations are noted as places of revelation where Jesus reveals himself in different ways. More important than place, however, is the recognition that Jesus discloses his identity best in relationship with others, even when the other is Satan:

1. In the wilderness
2. At the well
3. On the mountain
4. Along the road
5. At table
6. On the cross
7. On the road again

You, dear reader, could choose a litany of other stations that were important in Jesus' journey, but I have fixed on these as seven passages in the life and death of Jesus. In selecting them I was hoping I might make a crossover into people's lives, and that the issues that Jesus faced at these places might, in some way, speak to the challenges that you face in your own life.

It might be interesting for you to think of which seven stations would stand out on the journey of your own life: which places, in particular, have helped to define who you are today?

The main purpose of the book is to act as a personal companion for you for reflecting on the movement of the Jesus story. I hope that you might carve out some personal time for yourself and think about Jesus' journey and your own. How can the story of Jesus throw some light on your own story? And, conversely, how can reflecting on your own story throw some light on the Jesus story? The goal of this book is to promote a conversation between Jesus' journey and your own.

Each chapter of this book is written in five sections: in writing I wanted to provide a variety of resources for you to have at hand. Each chapter follows the following sequence:

- Introducing the theme
- The Gospel text
- Reflecting on the Gospel story, followed by a summary and prayer
- Meditation – a different angle and voice on the topic
- Questions for reflection, followed by a final prayer and blessing

I hope that you can, for a little time in your busy life, make a time of retreat for yourself, to think and pray about the journey of Jesus and the journey you are making in your own life. However the book is used, dear reader, I hope it proves somehow helpful to you.

Finally, I would like to say huge thanks to the young artist, Emma Blackwood, who kindly gave me permission to use five of her paintings to enliven the reflections. Her interest in the raw energy and vulnerability of the human body, together with the quiet strength of a body's soul, makes for its own series of reflections.

Sincerely,

Denis McBride C.Ss.R.
Alphonsus House
Chawton
Hampshire
GU34 3HQ

In the wilderness

Station One

In the wilderness

Sanctuary or wasteland?

Every country has them – the wastelands, the inhospitable regions, the uncultivated wildernesses, the badlands, the jungles, the swamplands. No-man's-land is everywhere, the unmapped terrain that most people naturally avoid, the bleak hostile territory where only the daring or the foolish venture. The wilderness, both as a place and as an archetype, has served a variety of purposes in the telling of the human story as:

- a place of refuge, a hideout
- a brooding, secret landscape
- a place of testing
- a sanctuary to escape the world
- a setting where you confront yourself
- a sacred place to meet God
- a godforsaken, wild place
- the territory of the devil
- the hinterland within
- the unconscious.

The image is weighted with ambiguity and goes in several directions. That said, however, the wilderness and the call of the wild both retain a powerful attraction for many people. In 1992, the young Christopher Johnstone McCandless, a brilliant academic student and elite athlete, walked alone into the wilderness in Alaska, north of Mount McKinley. After graduating with honours, he changed his name, gave the $24,000 he had in his bank account to charity, abandoned his car and possessions, and burnt the money he had in his wallet. He gave all this up to discover transcendent experience.

Chris McCandless had long admired the writer Leo Tolstoy, who had forsaken a life of privilege to wander among the destitute. Above all he admired the virtue of renunciation and wanted to live by this virtue, to test its limits in the wilderness. He lasted sixteen weeks (112 days) and eventually died of hunger. The writer Jon Krakauer spent over a year retracing that journey in his book *Into the Wild*, trying to uncover, from the journals kept by McCandless and speaking with his family, what made him fall in love with the wilderness. Six days before he died of starvation, aware of his plight, McCandless made the last entry in his journal: "I have had a happy life and thank the Lord. Goodbye and may God bless you all."[1] There is no regret that the wilderness he so much wanted to vanquish eventually destroyed him.

The wilderness enters the biblical story very early with Adam and Eve being

Journey · Wilderness · Well · Mountain · Road · Table · Cross · Road

banished from the Garden of Eden into the wilderness, and their son Cain being cursed and banned from tillable land to become a restless wanderer on the earth. The biography of the wilderness in the Bible ends with the book of Revelation when the woman clothed with the sun gives birth to a son, and is threatened by the red dragon that wants to consume her child: "the woman fled into the wilderness, where she has a place prepared by God" (Revelation 12:6). The biblical narrative moves between the two extremes: wilderness as exile and wilderness as security.

The Judean wilderness plays an important role at the opening of Jesus' ministry as the place of his initiation by John the Baptist and the scene of his temptations. An arid landscape of about 1,500 square metres, this wilderness occupies the area from the eastern slopes of the Judean Mountains down to the Great Rift Valley, running along the western shore of the Dead Sea, the lowest place on the surface of the earth. Very little rain falls here, so there are very few plants or animals to liven the landscape. Many deep wadis, formed by centuries of rain running off the hills, penetrate this wilderness.

As you can see from the picture, the Judean wilderness is no lush Lake District: it's an inhospitable, forbidding landscape – from a distance it resembles the highlands and the cratered surface of Mars. You're not going to go out there for a day's shopping or a cool picnic. The wilderness has a certain majesty about it, but – like a lot of majesty – it's not very attractive. Its bearing is too remote, the ground is too hard, the air is too thin, and the heat is too oppressive. There are too many rocks, too much light, too little life. Hence Jesus' question: "What did you go out to the wilderness to see?"

It was in the wilderness of Judea that David fled from the fury of Saul, that Elijah the prophet found sanctuary in its caves, and that

[1] Quoted in J. Krakauer, *Into the Wild* (London: Pan Macmillan, 2007), p. 198.

the Essenes escaped the priestly and temple domination of Jerusalem by settling at Qumran, near the Dead Sea. The wilderness is difficult to cross, which is why Herod the Great built two fortresses (Herodium and Masada) in the middle of the desert, as safe retreats in case the people revolted. Here John the Baptist led his revivalist movement and attracted the people of Judea and Jerusalem out to hear his message; it was here that John the Baptist and Jesus met for the first time. It was also here that the Zealots made their final desperate last stand against the might of Rome, at the fortress of Masada.

The Judean desert is known for its rugged landscape, which has provided a refuge and hiding place for rebels and zealots throughout history, as well as solitude and isolation for hermits. In later generations, after the growth of Christianity, monks began to inhabit the caves of the Judean wilderness and soon began building monasteries there, which clung perilously to the stark desert cliffs. In the Byzantine period, the wilderness attracted thousands of monks seeking seclusion, and by the sixth century there were about seventy monasteries spotted throughout the region.

The wild, untamed setting of the wilderness has also been used as an image for the unconscious, the unknown landscape that lies within each person. In traditional literature, the hero's departure from the safety of home and civilisation as he steps into the unknown is the first threshold of the adventure. When Odysseus leaves behind him the orderly life of the city state, Ithaca, his journey leads him to wilderness, to terrifying dark places where competing powers will test him. As he is challenged from without, he is also led within.

In his analysis of hero tales, *The Hero with a Thousand Faces*, Joseph Campbell stresses the role of the wilderness as symbolic of the unconscious:

> "The regions of the unknown (desert, jungle, deep sea, alien land, etc.) are free fields for the projection of unconscious content."[2]

The wilderness that challenges the hero from without is mirrored by the terrain of the unconscious which challenges him from within. His resolve will be tested not only in physical courage and endurance but in psychological stamina and mental resolve. Does he have the inner resources and the inner clarity to face the challenges that now beset him?

"Away, away, from men and
towns,
To the wild wood and downs,
To the silent wilderness,
Where the soul need not repress
Its music."
Percy B. Shelley
"The Invitation"

"I only went out for a walk and
finally concluded to stay out till
sundown, for going out, I found,
was really going in."
John Muir
The Mountains of California

"The trails I made led outwards
into the hills and swamps, but
they led inwards also. And from
the study of things underfoot,
and from reading and thinking,
came a kind of exploration of
myself and the land. In time the
two became one in my mind."
John Haines
*Twenty-five Years in the Northern
Wilderness*

Few of us would want the wilderness as our regular address. We prefer the familiar territory of our comfort zones, where we are in charge and can remain within the predictable rhythm of the familiar, unthreatened by any Satan. Sooner or later, however, we all find ourselves thrown into some sort of wilderness, within or without.

Some of us are thrown into the wilderness not by our own choosing but when our lives, without notice, are interrupted and we are suddenly faced with huge loss: a collapsed marriage, a lost love, financial disaster, sudden addiction. Sometimes wilderness is feeling utterly alone and unsupported, feeling abandoned by God or by those we love. Our prayer can become the lament of the God-forsaken: "My God, my God, why have you abandoned me?"

We ask, why did God allow this tragedy to happen to me? What did I do to deserve this? It's at times like these when we realise that we're not in control of our lives: we are no longer making things happen; rather, things are happening to us. And it's here, in the wilderness, that we search out ourselves and God. And we have to wait. Waiting can be its own wilderness.

After all, it took Jesus thirty years to reach the wilderness, a journey that was not his personal choice. The language of the narratives is in the passive voice ("led" – "thrust" – "expelled") indicating that Jesus was not the principal actor on this stage; the Spirit of God was directing him to the place of trial and testing, where from the outset of his ministry he would be questioned and forced to find clarity about himself and his purpose.

Sometimes you need your enemy to help you define who you are, what you stand for and what your governing purpose in life is. Sometimes, paradoxically, it can be your enemy that presses you towards resolution.

² J. Campbell, *The Hero with a Thousand Faces* (Princeton: Princeton University Press, 1968), p. 79.

Wilderness

Gospel text: Luke 4:1-13

Jesus, full of the Holy Spirit, returned from the Jordan and was led by the Spirit into the wilderness, where for forty days he was tempted by the devil. He ate nothing at all during those days, and when they were over, he was famished.

The devil said to him, "If you are the Son of God, command this stone to become a loaf of bread." Jesus answered him, "It is written, 'One does not live by bread alone.'"

Then the devil led him up and showed him in an instant all the kingdoms of the world. And the devil said to him, "To you I will give their glory and all this authority; for it has been given over to me, and I give it to anyone I please. If you, then, will worship me, it will all be yours." Jesus answered him, "It is written, 'Worship the Lord your God, and serve only him.'"

Then the devil took him to Jerusalem, and placed him on the pinnacle of the temple, saying to him, "If you are the Son of God, throw yourself down from here, for it is written, 'He will command his angels concerning you, to protect you,' and 'On their hands they will bear you up, so that you will not dash your foot against a stone.'"

Jesus answered him, "It is said, 'Do not put the Lord your God to the test.'" When the devil had finished every test, he departed from him until an opportune time.

Wilderness

Reflecting on the Gospel story

The setting

After Jesus is baptised by John the Baptist in the River Jordan, Luke tells us that he "was led by the Spirit into the wilderness". Mark's language is stronger: "immediately the Spirit drove him out into the wilderness" (Mark 1:12). Jesus is propelled by the Spirit into the Judean wilderness. This is not a decision that Jesus makes for himself: he doesn't decide to saunter into a quiet, expansive space to spend some time in retreat reflecting on his future mission; rather, he is thrust by the force of the Spirit into the wilderness to face a series of trials.

No one else in the Gospel witnesses this contest: we, the readers, are the privileged insiders invited to observe how Jesus is challenged and tempted. Although set in Palestinian geography, this is a cosmic stage where there is a battle between light and darkness, good and evil, Jesus and Satan.

It seems unlikely that this scene would ever have been "invented" by Jesus' followers. Given the belief in who Jesus is as Messiah and Son of God, you would not naturally move from that belief to the conviction that Jesus was tempted. Jesus' experience

of being tempted would appear to diminish the unique power of who you believe him to be.

On the other hand, if Jesus shared his experience of being tempted with his followers, that insight would become part of the Jesus tradition – as it does in three Gospels. The evangelist John has no story of Jesus being tempted: given his opening assertion that Jesus is the Logos who was with God and was God, it would seem inappropriate to narrate a scene where God is tempted.

Satan

Among the sons of God spoken of in Job 1:6-12, there is mentioned one, Satan, God's appointed "accuser". When God asks him where he has been, he replies, "Prowling about on earth, roaming around there." Satan is a member of God's council whose task is to test and accuse people – effectively he is God's prosecuting attorney. In the earliest literature Satan is not seen as God's opponent, but the divinely appointed patroller of the earth who tests and accuses particular people, reporting back to God on the outcome. It is only much later in Hebrew thought that the figure of Satan becomes an evil superhuman force, now

Journey   Wilderness   Well   Mountain   Road   Table   Cross   Road

opposed to God, now bent on enticing people to rebel against their creator.

The word "devil" (from the Greek *diabolos*, "slanderer") becomes interchangeable with Satan. Now there develops an understanding of two supernatural powers, God and Satan, good and evil, light and darkness. These two forces battle against one another on a cosmic stage; the earth itself becomes a battleground where that conflict is played out, although the belief is expressed that the light will never be overpowered by the darkness, and that Satan's final defeat will be accomplished by Christ on his final return.

In art it has always been a problem deciding how to depict Satan. From the Middle Ages he has been portrayed as an ugly monster, often with a horned head and cloven feet, an image, it has to be admitted, that now amuses more than terrifies. A master of disguise and deception, you could always recognise Satan in the medieval morality plays by his limp – a lasting defect from his fall from heaven.

When the writer and broadcaster Malcolm Muggeridge was making a BBC feature on the life of Jesus, he had to give serious thought about how to portray, on film, the image and presence of Satan in the desert. Eventually the production team decided to portray the presence of Satan as a shadow in the sand which lengthened as the exchange with Jesus developed. Muggeridge commented: "It may even have been Jesus' own shadow: dialogues with the devil have a way of turning out to be soliloquies."[3]

Temptation
Jesus is tempted. By definition a temptation has to be appealing, otherwise it would not be counted as a temptation: what tempts some people can appear repulsive to others. Are you ever tempted by what you

[3] I. Hunter (ed.), *The Very Best of Malcolm Muggeridge* (London: Regent College, 2003), p. 236.

find unappealing or unattractive? When we say, "I'm really tempted", we admit to the power of attraction that something holds out – or, more precisely, to some aspiration within us that feels it would be satisfied by doing it.

If Jesus was not really tempted, in what sense can we speak of the temptations of Jesus? It is an extraordinary and complex story – the idea of Jesus being tested and tempted.

> "We do not have a high priest who is unable to sympathize with our weaknesses, but we have one who in every respect has been tested as we are, yet without sin."
> (Hebrews 4:15)

In the three temptations Jesus never responds by himself; instead he quotes the book of Deuteronomy three times. Three times is not a coincidence – it is a deliberate device that points us back to Deuteronomy as the sourcebook that will serve to unravel this bewildering scene in the wilderness. Deuteronomy is the book of the Law and at the heart of this book there is the *Shema Israel* – the summary of the Law. This is the most important prayer that all Jews are invited to pray each day.

Interestingly it says, yes, three things.

> "Hear, O Israel: The Lord our God is one, the only God.
> You shall love the Lord your God with your whole heart, with your whole soul, with your whole might."
> (Deuteronomy 6:4-5)

This is the prayer the good Jew would pray morning and evening every day; it is a summary of the Law and a challenge to love God with one's whole being, so that no part of us is excluded from the fullness of that commitment to love. We love God even with our shadow side, even in the dark margins of our being, so that nothing in us is excluded from this act of unqualified love.

"You shall love the Lord your God with your whole heart."

First temptation: with your whole heart?

After forty days in the wilderness, Jesus is tempted to turn stones into bread. The Old Testament background to Jesus' temptations is Israel's experience in the wilderness. A new nation had been born, which God called his "son" (Exodus 4:22). After being miraculously delivered out of Egypt, the people were tested by God in the wilderness to see what was in their heart, whether they were wholehearted or not (Deuteronomy 8:2). Soon into their sojourn of forty years' wandering, the people of Israel became unhappy at Moses, who could offer them only manna, light food that appeared on the desert floor. Their hunger made them half-hearted about their new project of travelling to the freedom of the Promised Land.

They looked back at Egypt and nostalgically remembered the substantial food they ate there. Some preferred living under Pharaoh: they preferred the security that went with bondage to the hunger and pain that went with freedom. What would you prefer: being a slave on a full stomach in the land of Egypt or being free and hungry in the wilderness? Well-nourished bondage or poorly fed freedom?

The people were pulled in two directions: their commitment to the difficult road to freedom was being questioned in the light of their fresh hunger. Can you be ravenously hungry and still trust in God? Can you still follow God's way even when you are aware of the large vacancy inside you? Can you keep your heart undivided in the face of trial and need?

Later Jesus will preach: "Set your heart first on the kingdom of God." Firstly, ensure that your heart is undivided and set it on the kingdom. Jesus' own heart will be pulled in two directions – the direction his family want him to take and the direction his mission is leading him. Will he follow the family script or the mission directive? He will warn his disciples that they, in their turn, will be pulled in two directions as he was:

"As they were going along the road, someone said to him, 'I will follow you wherever you go.' And Jesus said to him, 'Foxes have holes and birds of the air have nests; but the Son of Man has nowhere to lay his head. To another he said, 'Follow me.' But he said, 'Lord, first let me go and bury my father.' But Jesus said to him, 'Let the dead bury their own dead; but as for you, go and proclaim the kingdom of God.' Another said, 'I will follow you, Lord, but let me first say farewell to those at my home.' Jesus said to him, 'No one who puts a hand to the plough and looks back is fit for the kingdom of God.'"
(Luke 9:57-62)

The disciples' hearts will be pulled in two directions: honouring the family and honouring the mission. Which will have priority? They will also be tested about food: "And do not keep striving for what you are to eat and what you are to drink, and do not keep worrying. For it is the nations of the world that strive after all these things, and your Father knows that you need them. Instead, strive for his kingdom, and these things will be given to you as well" (Luke 12:29-31). Again the emphasis is on an undivided heart that is wholly focused on the kingdom.

In the wilderness Jesus is pulled in two directions: answering his hunger or staying with the hunger for the sake of the mission. He resolves to keep an undivided heart: he will love the Lord and stay faithful to the mission even when his hunger cries out to be answered.

**Second temptation:
with your whole soul?**
In the second temptation Jesus is on a high mountain and Satan offers him all the kingdoms of the world. The devil offers Jesus immediate power if Jesus will worship him. Why follow a love you cannot see, with little to show for it, when you can have all the panoply of power now? Why not secure prestige and power now, with instant results, rather than the tedious route of gathering disciples and followers and winning them to your cause? How long will this venture take, and with what results? Better to surround yourself with the guaranteed trappings of absolute authority. You can have immediate status now – no need to wait – and you can lord it over kingdoms. All you have to do is acknowledge the lord of darkness.

Jesus will face this temptation to temporal power in his ministry. Remember when he feeds the five thousand in John's Gospel:

"You shall love the Lord your God with your whole soul."

the people respond by trying to kidnap him to make him their king, but he escapes back to the hills by himself. Jesus is not hungry for majesty, for domination, for political power: he flees from the offer of this immediate temporal power, from the temptation of instant sovereignty as king.

And he will warn his disciples about power and its use: "Do not lord it over others or make your authority felt." The authority that exalts itself and exults in itself has to be avoided. "You", he says, "must be servants."

Soon after the incident where Jesus calls Peter "Satan", the group heads for home, travelling through Galilee (Mark 9:30-37). Jesus has a second try at telling the disciples what is weighing down his heart: he tells them that he will be betrayed and put to death. Mark tells us how the disciples respond: they don't know what this talk of betrayal and death is about, and they are afraid to ask him. What Jesus wants to say, they don't want to hear, so they leave his revelation hanging in the air. They keep on walking and then choose their own topic to discuss, one that is much more important to them: they decide to move the discussion from Jesus' suffering to their own power.

The agenda for their group meeting is: which of them is the most powerful in the group?

Jesus walks alone. His revelation has separated him from his own group. They travel together, but separately. They leave Jesus to talk to himself.

Mark describes the scene with great sensitivity, and he invites us to imagine that awful return journey, a journey of some forty miles. Jesus is walking on ahead, isolated from the others, deep in his own thoughts, wondering why when he wants to be real with his friends he is left alone. His disciples follow at a safe distance, out of earshot, talking about what is important to them. Jesus and the disciples are on the same road but they are worlds away from one another.

When they get to their house in Capernaum Jesus asks them: "What were you arguing about on the way?" It didn't take long for their group discussion on power to end up in an argument about which of them was the greatest. Their fascination is for primacy, for hierarchy, for power. They didn't reach agreement about which of them was the greatest and they are now too ashamed to say anything; so nothing is said. The story moves from a road full of argument to a room full of silence.

Jesus breaks the silence to give a teaching to his disciples, these people fascinated by their struggle for power. He brings a child into the middle of the community meeting and says: "Whoever welcomes one such child welcomes me. Whoever wants to be first must be last of all and servant of all." Jesus allies himself not with his disciples and power, but with the child and powerlessness. The disciples are challenged to welcome littleness into their community. Their community is not to be an exclusive group reserved for the powerful; it is to be an inclusive community, where the little people can feel at home and they don't have to be bored to death by serious religious people discussing their own importance.

And this understanding is underlined, in John's Gospel, when Jesus takes it upon himself to demonstrate the upside-down nature of his kingdom by washing the feet of his disciples:

"Do you know what I have done to you? You call me Teacher and Lord – and you are right, for that is what I am. So if I, your Lord and Teacher, have washed your feet, you also ought to wash one another's feet."
(John 13:12-14)

By dressing as a servant and undertaking the servile and humiliating task of washing feet, Jesus identifies the paradoxical manner in which God chooses to reveal himself. The foot-washing episode parallels the account in Luke 22:27, where Jesus states: "I am among you as one who serves"; it also echoes the confessional hymn of Philippians 2:6-11, in which the Christ is described as one who "emptied himself, taking the form of a slave".

That idea of lowly service is a long way from Satan's offer of ruling over kingdoms. Do you base your kingdom on twelve shaky apostles or on the firm ground of real estate? Do you opt for a painless power over people or elect to walk the road of the suffering servant? Do you serve the Lord with what is available to you – that is, with your whole soul? Can Jesus do this?

Journey — Wilderness — Well — Mountain — Road — Table — Cross — Road

"You shall love the Lord your God with your whole might."

Third temptation: with your whole might?

In the third temptation Jesus is challenged to jump from the highest point in the temple and land unhurt – because the angels will arrive on time and save him from harm. There is no real danger in this exercise: it appears treacherous only to the uninformed spectator. Thus a spectacular swan dive from the heights that looks deadly dangerous ends up being a theatrical performance that never, for a moment, imperils the subject or involves pain or damage. In this temptation Satan makes a seductive suggestion: that it is possible to love God through theatrical gestures without enduring pain.

If any human being dives from the top of a building he or she can expect obliteration. This temptation faces the question of self-preservation. Are you prepared to face real pain and risk your life for the sake of the Gospel? Or do you avoid pain, fall back on your privilege and connections, and use your power to remain untouched by a fall that would destroy any human being? Can you endure only theatrical risk? Can you love the love that loves you, even when you are in real pain and you see your life slipping away? Can you still love God when you become a beggar, lying on the ground in Gethsemane, imploring God to take the cup of grief away from you? Can you still love God in the depth of your own pain and isolation even when you scream out, demanding to know why God has abandoned you?

There is a wonderful scene in J.D. Salinger's novel *Franny and Zooey*: Franny says that if a man is lying at the bottom of a hill with his throat cut, slowly bleeding to death, and if a pretty girl or an old woman should pass carrying a beautiful jug, balanced perfectly on top of her head, the dying man should be able to raise himself up on one arm and see the jug safely over the hill. When Zooey thinks this over, he gives a snort and says he would like to see this dying guy get interested in a beautiful jug.

The man with the slit throat sees the jug safely over the hill. This is a commitment to beauty wherever it manifests itself – no matter what condition we are in. The challenge is not to become self-obsessed even in the middle of our own dying, but to retain the capacity to look outwards, beyond the range of our own affliction and diminishment, and notice the beauty of a larger world.

Interestingly, Jesus will be tempted to avoid the road of pain by his own disciples. When Jesus speaks to them about his own future of pain, he tells them that the Son of Man must suffer many things, and be rejected by the chief priests and the elders and the scribes, and be killed. Peter then takes Jesus aside to protest against this kind of talk, this kind of future. But Jesus says to him, "Get behind me, Satan! For you are setting your mind not on divine things but on human things" (Mark 8:33). Peter is the only person in the Gospels that Jesus calls Satan, the accuser. This temptation – to avoid suffering – comes not from the devil in the wilderness but from Peter on the road to Jerusalem.

Jesus has to learn that loving God does not mean exemption from harm. He teaches us that we will be saved; he never tells us that we will always be safe. For Jesus the radical question is: will he continue to love God when his very life is in jeopardy? Will he be able to love God when his body is raised on the cross, and no angel will arrive in time to save him? Will he stubbornly love the Lord through suffering, rejection and even a violent death?

Summary

The temptations in the wilderness are a summary of the temptations Jesus will face throughout his ministry, right to the cross. They do not disappear after the wilderness. We, the readers, are introduced to them before the beginning of Jesus' ministry to help us understand what he will have to face throughout the remainder of his mission. He will struggle with these questions, as we struggle with them ourselves.

Can you love the Lord our God with your whole heart, even when you are hungry and forlorn and feel alone?

Can you love the Lord with your whole soul, even when you are powerless and fragile and have nothing to brag about before God?

Can you love the Lord with your whole might, even when you face danger and your very survival is threatened?

Jesus spent a life answering those questions. So, dear friends, will we.

Journey — Wilderness — Well — Mountain — Road — Table — Cross — Road

Prayer

O Lord God,
great is the misery that has come upon me.
My cares would overwhelm me,
I know not what to do.

O God, be gracious unto me and help me.
Grant me strength to bear what you send
and let not fear rule over me.

As a loving Father, take care of my loved
ones...

O merciful God, forgive me all
the sins I have committed against you
and against my fellow men.

I trust in your grace and commit
myself wholly into your hands.

So do with me as seems best to you
and as is best to me.

Whether I live or die, I am with you,
and you are with me, my God.

Lord, I wait for your salvation.

Dietrich Bonhoeffer

Wilderness

A woman at the National Gallery

Sometimes in the Gospel you see Jesus taking a short break from the demands of his ministry and the hungry attention of the crowds. You see him play hide-and-seek with the crowds, but he usually loses: the crowd seems to have a nose for his hideouts. Sometimes he goes to the other side of the Sea of Galilee, which was non-Jewish territory. The other side of the lake is his getaway, where he hopes that he and the disciples might be left in peace. But when he returns from his break the crowds press in and new demands are made on him. The holiday is over; it's back to business as usual.

When I lived at our pastoral centre in Hawkstone Hall, situated in the middle of expansive parkland in Shropshire, I would take a break usually in the city, usually in London. For me, the city was the other side of my lake. Normally I would go down to London for three days to see a bit of theatre and visit some art galleries, food for my soul.

Recently, during a break between lectures, I had a few days in London, trawling the galleries. I went into the National Gallery in London and spent time in my favourite section on Renaissance Italian paintings. After a couple of hours' looking, I thought I would have a bit of lunch downstairs in the restaurant.

It was very busy. I got the food and found a newly vacated table with two chairs, pleased that I had managed to get peace and protect myself from the madding crowd. I wasn't hungry for table fellowship. I'd just settled myself into my new comfort zone when a woman came up and pointed to the empty chair opposite me.

"Is anyone sitting there?" she asked.

My heart sank. I looked at the empty chair and had to admit the obvious, that there was nobody actually sitting in it.

"Oh, jolly good," she said, "I'm dying to sit down." She plonked her tray down and then arranged an assembly of packages beside her chair. When she sat down she let out a deep sigh and proclaimed to the room: "Art is tiring, isn't it? All that walking and looking. Exhausting, don't you think?"

I mumbled agreement and lifted my hamburger to have my first bite. She looked at what I was about to eat and announced, "I am a vegetarian myself."

Journey — Wilderness · Well · Mountain · Road · Table · Cross · Road

Dear God, I thought, what am I supposed to do with this piece of useless information? I looked at her plate piled high with rabbit food and I bit into the beast, somewhat guiltily.

She said, "I come up to town every week to go round a couple of galleries and look at paintings."

I said something about having a break for a few days to do the same.

"A break," she said. "A break from what? What do you do?"

I thought, O God, tell her you are a trainee serial killer and she might go away.

"I am a priest," I said.

"A priest? Really?" she said. "Gosh!" She looked at me: "You don't look like a priest."

"We come in all shapes and sizes," I said. I put more black pepper on my hamburger.

"I used to be religious," she said, "sort of, but I've given up on God. He's a bit of a disappointment, really. I mean he's never around when you need him – too busy sorting out the big bad world, don't you think?"

I called on all my years of theological training and said, "Yeah." I took another bite of the dreaded meat.

"You're agreeing with me," she said, looking disappointed.

I said, "Look, I'm no expert on God. He puzzles me as much as he puzzles you, and no doubt we return the compliment and puzzle him even more. We probably don't communicate well. We usually talk to God only when things are bad and our world is collapsing and we go screaming for help, madly hoping that he will make a difference. Distress telegrams are what God usually gets."

She smiled politely and tucked into her Spinach and Caesar salad, all the while measuring me with her eyes, which could puncture a battleship at a hundred yards. I watched all the healthy green food disappear into her healthy system. I was dying to escape for a smoke, but thought my new vegetarian companion would disapprove. I waited for her to finish so I could go.

She looked up and said, "I've just finished reading a wonderful book – twice – called *The Color Purple*. Do you know it?"

"Very well," I said. "A young friend of mine was studying it for her A levels, and she asked me to read it so we might discuss it together."

She said, "My favourite bit is when two of the characters are discussing God. One of them says something like, 'I think God gets mad, gets really mad if you walk past a field of purple and don't notice it. Everything, including God, wants to be appreciated. We, oh we sing and dance and talk and smile and give flowers, trying to be loved. Did you ever notice that trees do everything to get attention we do, except walk?'"

She laughed. "That's good," she said, "really sharp."

I said, "I remember that bit." And I looked at this woman for the first time and I saw a tree trying to walk, and I felt ashamed of my selfishness and my unwillingness to pay attention.

So I decided to stop looking at the exit and listen to her, this vegetarian stranger, as she talked about her miserable life and her miserable husband, and how they had settled into a wilderness world of sharing nothing but their common space. They had no children, four dogs, three servants, and a Grade I listed mansion, set in presidential grounds the size of Kensington Gardens.

For all their wealth and security, she said she felt like a plant you leave up in the attic to cheer up the room, but then you forget about it. Months later you come across the withered remains of what once was shining. "That's me," she said, "dried up, all dried up."

The spinach salad was finished.

She drank some mineral water.

She went on to tell me she came up to London to visit an art gallery one afternoon a week to look at paintings and borrow other people's dreams for a couple of hours. She would look at landscapes and faces, centuries old, paintings that commanded more attention in an hour than she would ever get in a lifetime.

I asked her what kind of painting she liked.

"Still life," she said. "I like still life paintings because they remind me of my own life. Nothing happening, really, just stillness. Things caught for ever, things that will never change, but in a funny way they have their own beauty. I love them."

I said nothing.

"Just imagine," she said, "what it would be like to be a famous painting for one afternoon of the world, and have all these people come to look at you and admire you and appreciate you. Oh, just imagine what that would feel like! Imagine the attention! I could feed off that for a lifetime."

I said, "Well, I have been with you longer than I have ever looked at a painting."

She looked at me with those eyes.

I looked away, around the restaurant, which was now almost empty. The crowd was gone, there were plenty of empty seats, plenty of space, plenty of still life.

"Can I see you again?" she asked.

"What would be the point?" I asked. "We live separate lives. It's been good talking to you, let's leave it at that."

She sighed, then rose from the table, adjusted herself, her hands smoothing what did not need to be rectified. "You will forget me, won't you?" she said.

"No," I said, "I won't. One day, I promise you, a church full of people will look at you like a still life. Just you. You won't know them or see them, but they will be looking."

She smiled and, with her collected parcels, walked away, without saying goodbye, back to her civilised wilderness. She left me sitting there with all the space in the world. I don't know who she was. When she left she wasn't aware, how could she be, of the small miracle she had performed – at table, in the National Gallery in London.

Wilderness

Questions for reflection

1. What has the woman in the National Gallery to do, if anything, with the story of Jesus in the wilderness?

2. Are there any temptations that have dogged you throughout your life? How have you managed facing them? Are you particularly vulnerable to a certain kind of temptation?

3. Being powerless is not an agreeable way of living in the world. We have a natural sympathy for people who are rendered powerless and helpless because they live in a totalitarian state and have no leverage to determine their own future. Why therefore did Jesus choose powerlessness?

4. Psychologists tell us that when it comes to understanding the hierarchy of human needs, the fundamental needs of people are for food, water and shelter. As Abraham Maslow commented: "It is quite true that man lives by bread alone – when there is no bread."[4] What would you say are your most basic needs?

5. How does the fact that Jesus was really tempted influence the way you think of him? Is being tempted a sure sign of weakness or simply an indication that you belong to the human race?

Final prayer and blessing

We pray for all those who are powerless
to influence their own future;
for all those who are oppressed
in body, in mind, or in spirit,
that whatever forces led them
to the crippling place they now live,
the Spirit might lead them
out of their address in the wasteland
and give them the courage and strength
to shape their lives anew.

We pray for all those who cannot resist temptation
and who, without intention, destroy their own lives
and bring distress and grief to their loved ones.

We pray for all those addicted to destructive behaviour:
that they might be granted the gift of insight
and the necessary power to choose life again
so they might enjoy peace and serenity in their souls.

We pray for ourselves:
that the Lord might not put us to the test
nor lead us to a time of trial,
but deliver us from all that is evil.

May the Lord mark us this day and all our days
with the blessing of his peace.
When we are tired and vulnerable,
may he enliven us with new purpose.
When we are unsure and distrustful,
may he fortify us with new confidence.
When we are depressed and weighed down,
may he raise us to new heights.
In all things, may his love be steadfast
and his care abiding.

This we ask in the name of the one he called Beloved,
Jesus Christ, our Lord.
Amen.

4 A. Maslow, "A Theory of Human Motivation", in *Psychological Review* 50 (1943), pp. 370-396.

At the well

Station Two

At the well

Connecting with people

What do you say after you say "Hello"? More basically, some people might ask, "How do you get to say hello to some people?" In a world where difference can often be seen as oddness, and where distinctness can be registered as estrangement, how do you go beyond the usual suspects and reach people totally different from you? The point about other people is that they are other. How do you devise a way of connecting with them, so that a conversation can begin? Or do you remain within the boundaries of your own limited world, connecting only with your "ain folk"?

Some individuals are approachable and easy to talk to, making you feel welcome and comfortable in their presence; others are shy and hesitant about what to say, but they gallantly struggle on, committed to the task at hand; others remain hopelessly distracted, looking over your shoulder, their eyes hunting the horizon for a more interesting prospect; others remain aloof, finding it difficult to contain their indifference, and when you do manage to talk to them, the exchange is so stilted and abrupt and leaden that you are left wondering why you bothered to make the connection in the first place.

Connecting with people is part of the ordinary round of everyday life. Few of us go through life without ever reaching out and joining some kind of group or club or association. Some people take pride in their membership of a whole range of different groups, from the local neighbours' association to rarer groups, like the British Society for the Protection of Hedgehogs. For some people, the more select the group – albeit the less other it is – the better they feel. You may remember Victor Mature, the American film actor who specialised in rather leaden romantic roles. He applied for membership to the exclusive Los Angeles Country Club. He was told: "We do not accept actors in this establishment." So Victor Mature wrote back protesting: "I am no actor, and I have sixty-four pictures to prove it." He may have been right, but he didn't get in.

Joining a particular group, religious or political or social, can enlarge our world and introduce us to new people and new possibilities. It can help us to move within a relatively secure network of relationships. That sense of belonging is important to our identity: membership is proof of how others accept and recognise us. Rejection is a clear signal of disapproval. As the

Scottish psychologist Professor David Smail observed:

"In order to function, we depend, throughout our lives, on the presence of others who will give us identity and validity. You cannot be anything if you are not recognised as something; in this way your being becomes dependent on the regard of other people."[1]

Gaining the respect of others, having them regard you favourably, is something that is important for most people – even though we live in an individualistic society, where who we are is defined by what we have made of ourselves. By contrast, in the ancient Mediterranean world, the family, not the individual, was the primary unit of importance and the psychological centre of life. Who you were was determined by your position in the family and the regard they and others had for you. Identity was family identity, not personal identity; individualism was shunned in favour of family loyalty.

If family solidarity was the primary social value in the ancient Mediterranean world, solidarity with the village came a close second. In a world where few people travelled regularly beyond the reach of the nearest market town, the family and the village set the geographical and emotional boundaries of the majority of people.

In the tightly knit agrarian community of the village, where you lived your life in close proximity to relations and neighbours, social conformity was a matter of survival, an essential part of maintaining self-esteem and "respect" within the close network of relations. Who you were was determined to a large extent not on how you regarded yourself but on how you were regarded in the eyes of your fellow villagers, whether you commanded their respect or not. To bring shame on the family was punished by exclusion.

[1] D. Smail, *Illusion and Reality: The Meaning of Anxiety* (London: Dent, 1984), p. 43.

You can see something of this dynamic in the parable of the prodigal son. On the return home of the younger brother, you watch the father reinstate his disgraced son into the community not by talking to him privately but by public gestures of welcome: the embrace, the kiss, the best robe, the ring, the sandals and the shared feast. This is not a private transaction but a public signal to everyone that the younger son should be welcomed back to the village in the same way that he is embraced and welcomed back by his father. That welcome and regard take away his shame.

In a small village a woman who has had five husbands, like the woman of Samaria, might be regarded as something of a sexual athlete and nonconformist or dismissed as someone who has a pathological incapacity to sustain relationships. Certainly her resolute ability to connect with men is equalled by her track record on disconnection: perhaps – who knows? – she was serially unlucky in her choices.

Whatever the case, she would have been treated with suspicion by the other villagers, particularly the women. Perhaps that is why she goes to the well at midday, when all the other women in the village would have gone in the cool of the early morning or evening, using the occasion to exchange news and gossip.

We watch the woman of Samaria as she goes to the well out of hours, and when she discovers a man there – the wrong kind, sadly, since he is a Jew – she instinctively tries to disconnect the conversation with him: he is too other. Some conversations are primed to go nowhere, marked as non-starters, because of the conflicting background of the speakers and the weight of inherited prejudice. This exchange appears to be one of them.

Journey — Wilderness — Well — Mountain — Road — Table — Cross — Road

Well

Gospel text: John 4:1-30. 39-42

Now when Jesus learned that the Pharisees had heard, "Jesus is making and baptizing more disciples than John" – although it was not Jesus himself but his disciples who baptized – he left Judea and started back to Galilee. But he had to go through Samaria. So he came to a Samaritan city called Sychar, near the plot of ground that Jacob had given to his son Joseph. Jacob's well was there, and Jesus, tired out by his journey, was sitting by the well. It was about noon.

A Samaritan woman came to draw water, and Jesus said to her, "Give me a drink." (His disciples had gone to the city to buy food.) The Samaritan woman said to him, "How is it that you, a Jew, ask a drink of me, a woman of Samaria?" (Jews do not share things in common with Samaritans.) Jesus answered her, "If you knew the gift of God, and who it is that is saying to you, 'Give me a drink,' you would have asked him, and he would have given you living water."

The woman said to him, "Sir, you have no bucket, and the well is deep. Where do you get that living water? Are you greater than our ancestor Jacob, who gave us the well, and with his sons and his flocks drank

from it?" Jesus said to her, "Everyone who drinks of this water will be thirsty again, but those who drink of the water that I will give them will never be thirsty. The water that I will give will become in them a spring of water gushing up to eternal life." The woman said to him, "Sir, give me this water, so that I may never be thirsty or have to keep coming here to draw water."

Jesus said to her, "Go, call your husband, and come back." The woman answered him, "I have no husband." Jesus said to her, "You are right in saying, 'I have no husband'; for you have had five husbands, and the one you have now is not your husband. What you have said is true!" The woman said to him, "Sir, I see that you are a prophet. Our ancestors worshipped on this mountain, but you say that the place where people must worship is in Jerusalem."

Jesus said to her, "Woman, believe me, the hour is coming when you will worship the Father neither on this mountain nor in Jerusalem. You worship what you do not know; we worship what we know, for salvation is from the Jews. But the hour is coming, and is now here, when the true worshippers will worship the Father in spirit and truth, for the Father seeks such

Journey — Wilderness — Well — Mountain — Road — Table — Cross — Road

as these to worship him. God is spirit, and those who worship him must worship in spirit and truth." The woman said to him, "I know that Messiah is coming" (who is called Christ). "When he comes, he will proclaim all things to us." Jesus said to her, "I am he, the one who is speaking to you."

Just then his disciples came. They were astonished that he was speaking with a woman, but no one said, "What do you want?" or, "Why are you speaking with her?" Then the woman left her water jar and went back to the city. She said to the people, "Come and see a man who told me everything I have ever done! He cannot be the Messiah, can he?" They left the city and were on their way to him…

Many Samaritans from that city believed in him because of the woman's testimony, "He told me everything I have ever done." So when the Samaritans came to him, they asked him to stay with them; and he stayed there two days. And many more believed because of his word. They said to the woman, "It is no longer because of what you said that we believe, for we have heard for ourselves, and we know that this is truly the Saviour of the world."

Well

Reflecting on the Gospel story

The setting

At the opening of this story the evangelist John tells us three times, lest we miss the point, that his scene is set not at any well, but at Jacob's well, the same well that Jacob, his sons and his cattle drank from, which is situated near the field that Jacob gave to his son Joseph.

Wells have played a key role in Hebrew culture, not least because, in an arid landscape where the rainfall is low, water is as important as air for nomadic people. Battles were fought over ownership of wells. Whoever owns the well is a keeper of life; whoever has access to the well has admittance to new life.

Like pubs and coffee houses, wells were natural gathering places, where news would be exchanged and the latest gossip gathered; they were also associated with romantic relationships. When Abraham is an old man, he commissions his chief steward to return to the old country and choose a wife for his son Isaac. When the steward reaches his destination, he sits down by a well and prays to God that as he asks one of the girls, "Please offer your jar that I may drink," she might respond, "Drink, and I will water your camels"

(Genesis 24:14). If the girl responds in this way, this will be a sure sign she is the chosen one. A beautiful girl named Rebekah – "whom no man had known" – comes to the well with her water jar and responds just as the steward had prayed. After securing her agreement and the blessing of her family, the steward takes her back to become Isaac's wife.

When Isaac's son, Jacob, flees home in fear of his brother, he heads for the land of his uncle Laban. On arrival he sees a well with flocks of sheep lying around waiting for water. When all the sheep are assembled, the shepherds will remove the stone and water them. Jacob asks the shepherds if they know Laban, and they reply that they do, pointing out that his daughter, Rachel, is approaching the well with her father's flock. On seeing Rachel approach, Jacob, without waiting for permission from the shepherds, eagerly removes the heavy stone by himself from the mouth of the well and then waters the sheep of Laban. This time the roles are reversed: it is the man who offers the water.

"Then Jacob kissed Rachel, and wept aloud" (Genesis 29:11). In this flood of emotion the speechless Jacob announces

his love for Rachel at the well – a love that will endure for the rest of their days. Jacob falls in love so deeply with Rachel that he is willing to work seven years for Laban to marry her – seven years that "seemed to him like a few days because of the love he had for her" (Genesis 29:20). As it turns out, Laban plants his elder daughter, Leah, in the marriage bed, and Jacob has to work another seven years to win Rachel. This he does as the first great romantic figure in the biblical narrative.

After Leah delivers four sons, her womb is closed; Rachel's womb does not open. Both women give Jacob a handmaiden to

extend the family line. Thus Jacob has two wives and two concubines: this great lover never had a cold night in his life! He fathers twelve children, so his name is changed to Israel, the father of the twelve tribes.

Rachel's womb opens out of season and she gives birth to a son, Joseph. He is different from his brothers: he loves technicoloured clothes and he can see in the dark what others cannot see in the light as an interpreter of dreams and decoder of night shadows. Eventually this useless, exiled dreamer will save his family from famine by bringing them down to Egypt. Later, when Jacob is on his deathbed, surrounded by all his family, he says to Joseph: "Now I am about to die… I give you a Shechem [Hebrew *shekem*, 'shoulder'] more than your brothers" (Genesis 48:21-22, *Jerusalem Bible*). It is this shoulder of land that is mentioned by John in the introduction to his story. We are in Jacob's country, at Jacob's well.

The encounter

Jesus, weary from his journey as he passes through Samaria on his way north to Galilee, has a midday break and sits down by a well near the ancient town of Shechem. When a Samaritan woman comes to draw water, he asks her for a drink: he is not only tired but also thirsty. It would have been regarded as inappropriate for Jesus, a solitary man, to engage a solitary woman in conversation – a point that is registered when his own disciples return to find them together and are shocked at what they see. Jesus seems unconcerned about infringing the rules of propriety: out of his need, he opens the conversation with this woman. Thirst knows no boundaries, submits to no cultural custom and makes no deference to political or religious affiliations. Thirst is a body yearning for a drink, no matter who you are.

The woman's instinct is to close the conversation by calling attention to the inherited differences between them. Rather than attend to the obvious – a thirsty man is beside her at a well and she has a water jar – she points out that they should not be speaking to one another because of the impediment of racial and religious difference. Sometimes raw human need becomes irrelevant beside the sheer weight of inherited prejudice; sometimes ethnic difference blinds people to the humanity of others and their neediness.

Jesus' response is not to debate their differences, but to intrigue her with the thought that if she knew his identity, she would be asking him for a drink, and – unlike her – he would not hesitate to give it. And this is not just still water from a well or cistern but living water. The woman counters with the observation that Jesus has no container with which to draw water from this deep well, so where will this living water come from? It was their shared ancestor Jacob, after all, who provided this well for his people: is this Jewish stranger greater than Jacob?

Jesus points out that anyone who drinks the still water provided by Jacob's well will become thirsty again, whereas anyone who drinks the water he gives will never thirst again because this water will become a spring inside, welling up to eternal life. Misunderstanding Jesus, the woman asks for this water, to save her from thirst and from the inconvenience of travelling out to the well at such a time, midday, one that marked her out as excluded and marginalised.

The conversation moves to a new level, focusing on her identity, when Jesus invites the woman to call her husband to join them.

When she replies that she has no husband, Jesus counters with the observation that she is right, since she has had five husbands and the man she currently lives with is not her husband.

In response, the woman's gradual reading of the stranger's identity comes to some clarity when she realises that this man is a prophet. But her instinct is to move away from the present topic – the arithmetic of her lovers – and focus on something less personal and troublesome, liturgical architecture. Highlighting difference again, she points out that her ancestors worshipped in the temple on Mount Gerizim while the Jews hold that the proper place to worship is in the temple in Jerusalem; she wonders which place wins out. According to the Jewish historian Flavius Josephus, the Samaritans had built their own temple on top of Mount Gerizim, a construction that provoked deep antagonism from the Jerusalem clergy. If the temple was the house of God, there could only be one such house on earth. Which temple was the proper place to worship God?

Neither place, says Jesus, for the hour is approaching when true worship of the Father will be in spirit and truth. Jesus returns to truth, something the woman has wanted to avoid, for how can you worship God if you avoid the truth? Worship is not about proper liturgical architecture; it is not about worshipping at the right address; it is not even about worshipping with the right crowd. It is about worshipping in spirit and truth.

Earlier on, in the episode of the cleansing of the temple in Jerusalem (John 2:13-22), Jesus replies to those who ask for a sign: "Destroy this temple, and in three days I will raise it up." The Jews misunderstand Jesus, pointing out that it has taken forty-six years to build the temple: how can he raise it up in three days? The evangelist John explains that Jesus is speaking about his body: the new temple is clearly identified as the resurrected body of Jesus. From this new temple will flow fountains of living water. This is the hour that is coming, when a new temple will be raised, rendering all previous temples pointless constructions. Only later will his disciples understand this saying.

In John's Gospel Jesus will define himself as the way, the truth and the life. Since God is Spirit, by definition we cannot see God, but this unseen God has sent his living Word among us: it is through this Word that we can come to know God in spirit and in truth. Through Jesus, the way is outlined, the truth is revealed and the life enlivens; through Jesus, all worship will be directed in the Spirit to the Father. We are no longer talking about buildings or architecture or animal sacrifice: true worship will be through a living body, the Word made flesh, in the person of Jesus.

The woman's understanding grows further as she responds by acknowledging the coming of the Messiah, the one who will show us all things. Jesus says, "I am he, the one who is speaking to you" (John 4:26). Jesus is seen to be God's self-revelation; he is seen to speak the truth. Through him the Father will be worshipped and glorified.

When the disciples return they have their own questions about their master speaking to a woman, but they say nothing, thinking the questions only to themselves. Meanwhile the woman leaves her water jar, a useless object, at the feet of Jesus and hurries back to the town. When she announces she has met a man, you can imagine her neighbours thinking, "Oh, not another one!" She defines this man in terms of truth, one who told her all she ever did,

appending the question: "Can this be the Christ?" Indeed, at Jacob's well, she has found one greater than her ancestor Jacob.

The power of witness

"Many Samaritans from that city believed in him because of the woman's testimony" (John 4:39). The words "testimony" and "witness" are key terms in John's Gospel, beginning in the Prologue where John (the Baptist) is introduced as the one sent by God: "he came for testimony, to bear witness to the light, so that all might believe through him" (John 1:7). In the other Gospels John the Baptist is seen as an independent figure who leads a revivalist movement, attracting Judea and Jerusalem out to listen to him in the wilderness. In the Fourth Gospel, however, John's vocation is clearly defined as giving testimony to Jesus. As F. Mussner notes:

"Testimony is given publicly. A witness usually appears in a law-suit and openly affirms what he has seen and heard. This public testimony by the witness has its own binding character."[2]

In that sense John's Gospel can be seen as a courtroom with the evangelist putting a case before the assembly "that you may come to believe that Jesus is the Messiah,

the Son of God, and that through believing you may have life in his name" (John 20:31). To argue his case the evangelist calls a number of witnesses to the stand, John being the first witness to testify. But John is not the only witness to give evidence in the evangelist's courtroom:

- Jesus bears witness to what he knows and has seen (3:11)
- The woman of Samaria witnesses to her own town (4:7-42)
- The works that Jesus performs bear witness to him (5:36)
- The Father bears witness to Jesus (5:37; 8:18)
- The scriptures bear witness to Jesus (5:39)
- Moses witnesses to Jesus in his writing (5:46)
- Jesus can bear valid witness to himself (8:14)
- The Spirit of truth will bear witness to Jesus (15:26)
- The disciples are qualified to be witnesses to Jesus (15:27)
- The evangelist himself bears witness to Jesus (19:35; 21:24)
- The evangelist's school, in turn, bears its own witness (21:24)

As a witness, the woman of Samaria testifies from her own experience. She speaks out of the authority of her own experience: she is not sharing her thinking or her ideas, but her experience. To speak about Jesus she consults her own story, not a book, not a scholar and not a school of thought. The jury must decide whether she is worthy of belief and accept or reject her testimony.

The evangelist John is taking a mighty risk in presenting this woman as a witness – not only because across the ancient world the word of a woman was not accepted as testimony in a court of law, but because the word of this particular woman, given her moral background, would not secure automatic respect from any jury. You can imagine what an effective counsel for the prosecution would do to her and her testimony in a witness box. Yet the extraordinary thing is that the evangelist includes her in his gathering of witnesses, a measure of his confidence in a woman who has already won over a town by the strength of her testimony.

The woman's testimony leads the townspeople to seek Jesus out at the well for themselves, which they do, and Jesus stays with them for two days. The townspeople have the opportunity to experience Jesus for themselves and so they say to the woman: "It is no longer because of what you said that we believe, for we have heard for ourselves, and we know that this is truly the Saviour of the world." In their turn, the townspeople become witnesses. They can proclaim, in the language of the first letter of John:

[2] F. Mussner, *The Historical Jesus in the Gospel of St John* (New York: Herder & Herder, 1967), p. 36.

"what we have heard, what we have seen with our eyes, what we have looked at and touched with our hands, concerning the word of life – this life was revealed, and we have seen it and testify to it, and declare to you".
(1 John 1:1-2)

Anyone who has experience can, if they reflect on it, become a witness. Those who had experience of new life in the Gospel converted their experience into a message. They described what happened: their experience became a story, opening up new possibilities for others. Their experience is not just a personal story of change; it leads them to make claims about Jesus. Given what happened to me, who then is he? What does my experience say about him?

John underlines the role of experience in understanding Jesus; the pastoral purpose of this is to bring people into a community of faith. Jesus shared his dreams with those who knew him, hoping their relationship with him would become Gospel. The Gospel begins when we have a living relationship with Jesus. It is thus that the Gospel is preached, thus the tradition is handed over, thus the community grows in faith.

If you were on the parish council, interviewing for a new teacher for adult religious education, and the woman of Samaria applied for the job, how would you respond to her colourful curriculum vitae? Would she have a chance at the job? Or would it be a case of a hurried, "Next, please!"

Summary
Jesus waits alone at the well of Jacob, in Samaria; a lone woman from the district arrives, to collect water, and when Jesus asks her for a drink she reminds him why they should not be relating. Jesus persists, gradually questioning the woman while at the same time revealing himself to her. Two revelations meet at the well. The woman returns to her town and turns her experience into a story, becoming one of the first witnesses to Jesus in the evangelist's courtroom drama. Her testimony is effective, leading the townspeople to meet Jesus for themselves, many of whom come to belief in him.

Journey — Wilderness — Well — Mountain — Road — Table — Cross — Road

Prayer

Now it is you alone that I love,
you alone that I follow,
you alone that I seek,
you alone that I feel ready to serve
because you alone rule justly.

It is to your authority alone
that I seek to submit.

Command me, I pray,
to do whatever you will,
but heal and open my eyes
that I may hear your voice.

Drive out from me
all fickleness,
that I may acknowledge you alone.

Tell me where to look
that I may see you,
and I will place my hope
in doing your will.
Amen.

St Augustine

Well

Meeting Jesus from Alabama

**Sometime this week, give yourself five minutes alone.
Sit quietly; be still. Imagine yourself sitting in a cafe;
there are no other customers. You are alone.**

So, there you are, eyes cast down,
looking into your cup,
foraging for pattern in what is left,
as if your cup were a deep well
that might vouchsafe to you
your fortune or fate.
Everything, you believe, is in the tea leaves,
the leftovers of what you've supped.
Oh, you know it's only a cup,
but it's a way of passing the time, isn't it?
After all, time is something to be endured.

You make that cup of tea last for ever, don't you?
Each sip – you have measured them, I know,
fourteen to the cup – is like a slow deliberate
station of the cross, heading, unmistakably, for exit.
You hate it when the cup is empty
and your devotions are ended,
and you have to rise and go back.

Was it T.S. Eliot who wrote that line?
I have measured out my life with coffee spoons.

The owner of the cafe, Harry himself, is kind:
he never hurries you or bothers you; never fusses.
By now he knows that you come here to be alone,
the only regular on a Friday night, to his cafe,
to drink the longest cup of tea in the world.
He stays out of the picture,

happy to be of some service to a fragile soul.
Never an inquisitive man
in this city of strangers and immigrants,
he is happy to let be whoever graces his tables.
He would love, however, to know your name,
only that he might be able
to welcome you and say his goodbye
on a more personal note.

Suddenly
the door opens,
the old-fashioned bell above the door jingles,
announcing an arrival or a departure.
It must be an arrival
for there is no one but you to depart.

You decide to look up from your cup
and turn your head to the doorway on your right:
you see a man enter.
Immediately, without hesitation,
without knowing how,
you recognise this man to be Jesus of Alabama.

He closes the door behind him.
He is alone – no disciples following in his wake,
no emergency-ward trailing after him,
no screamers demanding attention.
Alone he turns away from the closed door
and steps into your sanctuary,
into your chosen place of retreat.
And he comes to Harry's Cafe
not because he is thirsting after a drink
but because he is yearning to hear your story.

You sense this, somehow; this you know.
He is coming here, all the way from Alabama,
to meet you. You, among all the people in this city,
are his destination, his journey's end.

There are plenty of empty chairs around,
but, as you guessed,
he chooses the one opposite you.
He first asks you politely if there is anyone sitting there.
You look, as if to check, smile politely and say no.
He sits opposite you, facing you and the dark.

What to do?

You are tempted to look at your watch and say,
"Gosh, look at the time!
Lord, I really must run.
I really need to be somewhere."

But from somewhere inside
another voice tells you:
Do not be afraid.
There is no need to run.
There is no need to pretend.
There is no need to be someone you are not.
Be yourself.
Wait, wait, wait.
He knows the mystery of you.

You decide to risk staying put.
But you're nervous,
for no one has ever shared your table
at Harry's Cafe.

He looks at you.
He smiles.

You manage a smile back.
He shivers a little. "Cold," he says.
You nod in polite agreement.

He looks past you,
out through the window behind you.
"The nights are drawing in," he says.
"Dark out there now."

You say, "Right",
almost smiling to yourself at his awkwardness,
thinking the question you think often:
What do say after you say hello?

Then he says,
"I've been pacing up and down outside,
across the street, this Shabbat night,
and noticed you sitting here alone,
with only your cup of tea for company.
I'm not a voyeur, believe me, or anything like that.
I felt somehow that I couldn't just look and pass by,
that I had to come in."
He stops for a moment as if to review what he's said,
shrugs his shoulders, and admits,
"Sounds a bit witless, I know."

He looks around,
inspecting the empty room
as if some answer will emerge from the shadows.

"Forgive me," he says,
"I have no right to impose myself on you,
no right to intrude into your life,
but I'm dying to ask you:
Why do you come here?
Why do you sit here for so long?
Who or what are you waiting for?"
He takes the cup and saucer from your hand
and places them gently
in the middle of the white marble table-top.
Both of you can see the cup is empty.
You become aware of Harry, the owner,
looking at you from across the counter,
awaiting your instructions to intervene.
Unsure what to do, he comes across
and asks your table-companion
if he would like to order something.

"Please," the reply comes,
"I'm really thirsty. A pot of tea for two, thanks."
Harry looks at you and you smile your consent.
"Coming up," he says as he clears the table.

Jesus from Alabama turns back to you and says,
"Haven't had tea for two in a long while."
For some reason he smiles broadly
as if recalling some secret memory.
Then, leaning in to the table, he asks his question:
"Tell me, what do you really thirst for?
What do you thirst for
more than anything in the world?"

From somewhere outside
you hear a dog barking;
you hear the distant rumble of a subway train;

you can even hear the dark
pressing against the huge windows.
Suddenly your ears are finely tuned to
the world outside Harry's Cafe.

You listen.

Harry shuffles over, coughing to announce
his arrival, bringing a tray with a large white pot of tea,
two cups and saucers, a milk jug, a sugar bowl,
and a plate holding two complimentary biscuits.
Placing them on the table, he says, "Enjoy",
and returns behind the counter, to the far end,
to watch this little drama act out,
remaining protective of his regular customer.

Jesus busies himself
pouring out two cups of tea,
placing a cup in front of you.

He waits,
aware of the burden of his questions.

After what seems an age,
he brings you back into the room,
back to the table,
back into the sound of yourself.

"I'm here," he says.
"Talk to me.
Tell me about your home place
and about why you left.
Tell me how you are.
I'm not going anywhere.
I'm listening.
I have all the time in the world."

Well

Questions for reflection

1. If you were sitting at a well alone, or at a table in an empty cafe, and noticed Jesus approaching, what would you do? How would you feel? What would you want to say to him?

2. Are there any individuals or groups of people that you would never dream of talking to? Why not?

3. Given the woman of Samaria's background, how effective, for you personally, would she be as a witness? Would her background annul her testimony?

4. Who are the kind of people you would automatically dismiss as people unworthy of being heard? How would you rate yourself as a Christian witness?

5. We name people according to our experience of them: given your experience of Jesus, what name would you give him?

Final prayer and blessing

We pray for all who are marginalised in life,
for all who are excluded because of their race,
their religion, or their gender:
that they might know the loving embrace of the Lord
who offers them living water,
and experience the acceptance of the community.

We pray for all minorities in every land
who struggle to maintain their own customs
and safeguard their traditional lands.
That they might be seen as a blessing, not a threat;
a gift to the nation, not an embarrassment.

God and Father of all creation,
we bless your holy name,
which you revealed through the Word
you sent among us, your eternal gift,
Jesus Christ, our Lord and God.

He is the way:
through him may we know you and worship you.
He is the truth:
may he reveal your loving plans to us.
He is the life:
may he bring life in its fullness to our lives.

May the God who revealed his fullness in Jesus
bless us and keep us close;
may he never withdraw his love from us,
but remember us as the brothers and sisters of Jesus.

This we pray through Christ our Lord.
Amen.

On the mountain

Station Three

On the mountain
Mirror image

An old cryptic Chinese saying observes, "You cannot transfigure yourself." I presume it means that something must happen to you or, better still, someone must happen to you, to make you clearly change for the better, so that now you look radiant, shining and more alive. Something is showing through that wasn't showing through before. Your visible change leads people to wonder. When you walk into a room people notice a difference about you; some might ask, "Whatever happened to you?" The presumption is that something must have happened to you; that you did not organise this transformation yourself; something must have come over you.

The growing industry of cosmetic surgery is built on the belief that you can set up your own transfiguration: all you need is a reliable surgeon to carry out your instructions – a delicate nip here or a generous tuck there – and you will be visibly improved.

Living in a society obsessed with appearance and reflection and image, many people worship before the shrine of the mirror while acknowledging regularly before their god that they will never measure up to expectations. Mirrors are the

last confessionals. As Ernestine Northover noted somewhat wryly:

> "Mirror, mirror on the wall,
> Why do I look in you, at all,
> For all I see is the same old me,
> And not how I so want to be."

There are magazines aplenty, some needing the support of exclamation marks in the title, dedicated to displaying flawless images of celebrity and beauty and youthfulness. Every image leaks success, privilege, affluence; there is no hint of hardship or struggle; in this world of impressions everyone and everything glitters. With every shining page you turn, your own ordinary life, by comparison, seems duller and more uneventful until eventually, by the final section on Hollywood gossip, you feel you have been dismissed into oblivion.

In ancient days, people used to read the lives of the saints for inspiration, hoping they might grow wise by learning from the saint's dedication and improving themselves by imitating the saint's virtue or way of life. Hagiographies have been cancelled in favour of glossy magazines that offer new heavenly bodies of stars to

be idolised and adored, but hardly, it has to be said, imitated. The regular weekly devotion is to the fleeting image, the flashing smile, the flickering glamour. Like eating junk food, however, the satisfaction is momentary.

While images of Jesus abound in the pages of the Gospel, paradoxically no accurate picture can be formed of him: there is no mention of his physical appearance or the personal details that would be needed to form a reliable likeness of him. Given their subject and their unconcealed devotion, the evangelists are remarkably free of celebrity worship.

There is one passage, however, that focuses on Jesus' appearance – when something happens to him on a mountain top and he becomes radiant in the presence of his disciples. We call it the transfiguration of Jesus.

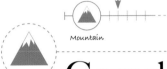

Mountain

Gospel text: Luke 9:28-36

Now about eight days after these sayings Jesus took with him Peter and John and James, and went up on the mountain to pray. And while he was praying, the appearance of his face changed, and his clothes became dazzling white. Suddenly they saw two men, Moses and Elijah, talking to him. They appeared in glory and were speaking of his departure, which he was about to accomplish at Jerusalem. Now Peter and his companions were weighed down with sleep; but since they had stayed awake, they saw his glory and the two men who stood with him. Just as they were leaving him, Peter said to Jesus, "Master, it is good for us to be here; let us make three dwellings, one for you, one for Moses, and one for Elijah" – not knowing what he said. While he was saying this, a cloud came and overshadowed them; and they were terrified as they entered the cloud. Then from the cloud came a voice that said, "This is my Son, my Chosen; listen to him!" When the voice had spoken, Jesus was found alone. And they kept silent and in those days told no one any of the things they had seen.

Journey — Wilderness — Well — Mountain — Road — Table — Cross — Road

Mountain

Reflecting on the Gospel story

Disfiguration

When we hear the word "transfiguration" in a religious setting, most of us immediately think of this dramatic story, set on a mountain top, of the transfiguration of Jesus. We think of transfiguration as something that happened to Jesus while he was at prayer, an extraordinary experience witnessed by his inner council, Peter, James and John. Yet transfiguration is a much wider theme in the Gospels; indeed it is one of the principal marks of Jesus' ministry.

Remember the scene when John the Baptist, confined in prison, sends his own disciples to ask Jesus the question: "Are you the one who is to come, or are we to wait for another?" When John's disciples find Jesus, they discover him at work, and they can see how his work focuses on the disfigured people.

"Jesus had just then cured many people of diseases, plagues, and evil spirits, and had given sight to many who were blind. And he answered them, 'Go and tell John what you have seen and heard: the blind receive their sight, the lame walk, the lepers are cleansed, the deaf hear, the dead are raised, the poor have good news brought to them.'"

(Luke 7:21-22)

In this passage Jesus' ministry is clearly summarised in terms of transfiguration: through the power of God at work in him Jesus rebuilds those who are broken, restores those who are wounded and brings good news to those who are overburdened, so that their best selves are freshly revealed. Throughout his public ministry Jesus is followed by crowds of people desperate for transfiguration – for healing, for forgiveness, for acceptance. In the pages of the Gospel you never once see Jesus embarrassed by people, however disfigured or deformed they might be; rather, he seeks them out as the focus of his mission: "Those who are well have no need of a physician, but those who are sick. I have come to call not the righteous but sinners to repentance" (Luke 5:31-32).

Think for a moment: how would you like to be transfigured? What would it take to transform you so that you would look radiant and aglow, exuding new life? What would have to happen to you to bring about that change?

When we think of our own transfiguration we tend to focus on something that is wrong in our lives, some distortion in our personality that could benefit from

treatment or some ancient wound that needs healing. If, for instance, you felt hopelessly unappreciated in your life and work, transfiguration for you might be the experience of your family and fellow workers holding you in high regard, thus making you feel worthy and worthwhile. In that new experience of their genuine estimation you would walk differently; you would look at the world from a new vantage point.

In the parable of the Last Judgement, in Matthew 25, we learn that just as we all have the capacity to disfigure people – by ignoring them – we also have the capacity to transform them – by attending to them. Matthew introduces us to different groups – the hungry, the thirsty, the naked, the estranged, the sick and the imprisoned – a litany of people defined by their hardship or destitution, all longing for others to attend to their plight and transfigure them with mercy and kindness.

And the people who are welcomed into the fullness of the kingdom are not superstars who have performed spiritual heroics, but ordinary folk who have paid attention to the plight of their brothers and sisters. The blessed are commended for their actions, not their attitudes; for what they did, not for what they thought. Misery obliged them to act, so their active verbs prove to be what is important. Their response was humane and, therefore, profoundly religious; it is hallowed as the kingdom response of those who take responsibility for a broken world. They inherit a kingdom because they paid attention and transfigured others by their kindness.

There is a sense in which disfiguration defines transfiguration as, for example, can be seen in the list below.

Disfiguration	Transfiguration
sick	healed
caught up in habit of sin	released, forgiven
lost sense of direction	found
possessed by evil for destruction	self-possessed, in charge
unwanted, unloved	wanted, loved
estranged, unwelcome	accepted, welcomed
unnamed and unknown	named and known

61

Throughout his ministry Jesus is seen to transfigure people, liberating them from a world where their deformity or sin defines who they are. And the day comes when Jesus is transfigured himself by the Father who loves him.

The setting

In Luke's Gospel the first narrative of Jesus' public ministry concludes with a strange incident: his own townspeople of Nazareth take Jesus from the local synagogue and then try to kill him by throwing him from a nearby hilltop. That violent rejection on a hilltop in Nazareth is dramatically reversed when Jesus later climbs to the higher hilltop of Tabor and receives the loving acceptance of his Father.

The whole account in the Nazareth synagogue moves from quick admiration through sour disapproval to violent rejection. Everyone in this village in the hills of Galilee would have known Jesus. According to the Benedictine archaeologist Bargil Pixner, "The excavations during recent decades have shown that the population of Nazareth at the time of Jesus could hardly have numbered more than 120-150 people."[1] The local people who knew Jesus as the son of Joseph are being asked to accept a new Jesus, the one who now communicates with the power and authority of a prophet.

The experience of disfiguration that Jesus undergoes at the hands of his own people can be dramatically juxtaposed with his experience of transfiguration on the mountain: on this summit he hears his name called in love, and that experience of fatherly approval radically changes him. Where Nazareth says no, Tabor says yes; where Nazareth leads Jesus only to run away, Tabor leads him to set his face towards an ancient appointment in the city of Jerusalem.

Geographically, the graceful outline of Mount Tabor makes for a dramatic landmark in Lower Galilee, one that can be seen from miles around. Unsurprisingly, Tabor has been popularly chosen as the traditional place for the transfiguration not least because it is the highest summit in the region, the nearest to the heavens. When you stand on Mount Tabor you can look north-west across the valley and look down on the hills surrounding Nazareth: acceptance dominates rejection; love outflanks violent disapproval.

Situated in the north-west corner of the Jezreel Valley, Mount Tabor rises steeply and majestically to a height of 1,938 ft (588 m) above the plain below. From various perspectives, the mountain appears to stand prominently on its own (see picture above), but it is connected by a low saddle with the hills to the north-west. An outstanding landmark, it can be seen from great distances; its visual splendour, in the shape of a perfect breast, and its aura of the sacred have always evoked admiration and wonder: "Tabor and Hermon joyously praise your name" (Psalm 89:12).

The large plateau on the top of the mountain has the appearance of nature's sacred space inviting people to worship, which they have done from earliest times. If a mountain provides the highest earthly contact with the heavens, Mount Tabor has no contest from the surrounding area as the prime sanctuary. In the second millennium BC there was a Canaanite shrine, a High Place, on top of Mount Tabor; it was dedicated to the worship of Baal, the god of time, of fertility and of war.

On account of its graceful form and the splendour of its panorama, it is of little surprise that ancient tradition held Mount Tabor as "the high mountain apart" (Mark 9:2) of the transfiguration, although the canonical Gospels do not specify the location.

Two challenges facing Jesus

Before Jesus climbs the mountain, there are two outstanding challenges he has to face. The first concerns the growing opposition to his mission, led by the religious authorities of his day, the chief priests and scribes, a hostility that seems determined to put him to death. How can Jesus continue in the direction his mission is leading him when the prospect of his early death has shifted from the probable to the inevitable? The second challenge Jesus faces, following his rejection in Nazareth and discovering how the crowds identify him, is about how he is regarded by people: "Who do people say I am?" If no one knows your true name or recognises your real identity, how can you succeed with your declared mission?

In the first challenge Jesus has to decide which voice he listens to: the voice outside, coming from the official religious leaders, stating that he is a fake and an agent of the devil, misguiding the people and perverting the tradition of the ancestors; or the voice inside, which directs him in the choices he makes and the people he cherishes.

Think for a moment. If you, a good Christian, honestly believed that God had given you a mission in life, but you also

[1] B. Pixner, *With Jesus through Galilee according to the Fifth Gospel* (Rosh Pina: Corazin, 1992), p. 15.

knew that the country's hierarchy was united in opposing you, which voice would you listen to? The religious authorities are unanimous in their belief that you are making the wrong choices and leading people astray. As a good Christian, you have been educated in the belief that the hierarchy speaks with God's authority and that their judgement should be treated with respectful obedience. Their official estimation of you and your mission is on a collision course with your own understanding, and that awareness will inevitably throw you into inner conflict. The voice within you says: "This is the work God wants you to do." The official voice says: "We are going to put a stop to you."

What do you do? Which voice do you follow?

Jesus has to make up his mind whether he is going to listen to his personal inner voice, or the official outer voice. If he continues to follow his inner voice, it will surely lead to his death. Jesus will not die of natural causes; he will not die of old age; he will not die in his bed: he will, if he continues, be put to death in a most ugly, violent way. No one would embrace that way of dying without due cause.

Jesus recognises that the religious authority is desperately determined to maintain stability among the people and oversee the orthodoxy of teaching while ensuring the tradition remains sacred. Someone who destabilises the status quo, who openly criticises religious authority, will clearly pose a threat to the time-honoured conventions of the regular life. Moreover, someone who sets himself up as the authentic religious authority ("Come to me, all you that are weary and are carrying heavy burdens, and I will give you rest") while dismissing the standing authority as oppressive and pastorally useless ("Woe to you… for you load people with burdens hard to bear, and you yourselves do not lift a finger to ease them") is heading for inevitable conflict and opposition.

The religious authority decides early on in the ministry of Jesus that, for the sake of the community, Jesus has to go. The high priest Caiaphas' argument is not that of a pathological thug, but the argument of a religious leader, concerned for the well-being of the faithful. The high priest will conclude his considered judgement by stating that, on balance, it is expedient that one person should be dismissed to ensure the peace of the community.

(It might be worth noting that, some time later, you will see the early Christian leadership in Jerusalem make a similar judgement on the upstart Paul: up to the arrival of Paul in the city, the local community were living in peace; with the preaching of Paul, there came turmoil and death threats. The disciples act quickly, take Paul to Caesarea, put him in a boat and send him back home to Tarsus: one man is dismissed for the sake of the community. After Paul's dismissal, Luke states: "the church throughout Judea, Galilee, and Samaria had peace" [Acts 9:31]. For the sake of peace, the Christian community will follow the example of Caiaphas, albeit without violence, in dismissing those who upset the harmony of the community.)

If the religious hierarchy of Jesus' day are truly God's people, God's constituted authority, then why is God, ruler of all things, allowing his chosen leaders to arrange Jesus' disappearance and death? How can you connect your mission from God with your death by God's agents? Would not the prospect of being put to death – not by a lonely assassin but by official authority – appear to cancel out your mission? You can see this very judgement being made by the two disciples of Emmaus in Luke 24: "we had hoped that he was the one to redeem Israel". Why did they discard this hope, dismissing it to the past-perfect tense? Their hope died because "our chief priests and leaders handed him over to be condemned to death and crucified him". Jesus' own disciples believed that his death cancelled his mission.

In the second challenge, focusing on his identity, Jesus will risk the question, before he climbs the mountain, inviting his disciples to report on who people think he is, then challenging them to answer the same question. It is always risky to invite the evaluation of others by asking them who they think you are, not least because the answer you hope to receive is probably not the answer you will hear. Rather than risking the question, "Who do you say I am?" we are more likely to be heard saying, "Who do you think you are?" If no one knows your name or your true identity, then inevitably that experience will hurt you and diminish you.

The report of the disciples – that people perceive Jesus to be John the Baptist or Elijah or one of the prophets – is not an answer calculated to excite. How would you feel if you were told you were an old prophet having another go at things? Do the answers Jesus hears drive Jesus to climb the mountain and commune with God in prayer?

However Jesus thought of himself during his ministry, we have no account of that in the Gospels. Since none of the Gospels was written at the time of Jesus' ministry, recording events as they happened, we have to read them as reflections on the significance of who Jesus is for them – which is why the scripture scholar James Dunn has entitled his opus on Jesus as *Jesus Remembered*.[2] The Gospel writings reflect the estimation of the Christian community about who they believe Jesus to be at the time of writing: the Gospels reflect the community's faith in who Jesus is; they do not report on how Jesus thought of himself during his ministry. Everything they write about Jesus is written through the lens of their faith in Jesus as Lord.

That said, it seems clear that, given the dangerous path Jesus elected to walk and the radical choices he made, he must have had a strong sense of his identity, a sure sense of his own authority and an unwavering understanding of what his mission involved. Insecurity about your identity and direction do not easily graduate into a clear sense of your own authority and a stubborn determination to take a specific road in life. However deeply you understand your own identity and direction, it is difficult to hold on to that sense of yourself when it is not recognised or shared by others. We need others to confirm us in who we are; we need other voices to validate our identity. And, for Jesus, that validation is at the heart of the transfiguration account.

The two answers that Jesus receives

In the structure of the transfiguration account, there is a simple element and a wonderful element. In the simple element Jesus goes up a mountain, taking with him his three favourite disciples, Peter, James and John. His stated purpose in going up the mountain is not to manifest himself to his disciples but to pray. During his prayer something happens to him; he visibly changes while he prays, becoming radiant and aglow.

When you watch someone praying, how do you know what is going on? You don't know, unless they later share their experience with you, telling you, "I got an answer to my prayer." When you hear

them relate the answer to their prayer, you don't have to be a genius to work out what was the problem, what was the question that drove them to pray in the first place. If people say, "This is the answer to my prayer", then you go through the answer to work out what was the critical question.

Simple element: the event	Wonderful element: the significance
(a) Jesus goes up the mountain with three chosen disciples, in order to pray.	(a) Two men appear, Moses and Elijah, and speak of how Jesus' departure (exodus) will be accomplished in Jerusalem.
(b) While he is at prayer, Jesus changes, becoming radiant and aglow. This is seen by his disciples.	(b) The voice of God declares: "This is my Son, my Chosen One; listen to him!"
(Jesus clearly has an answer to his prayer. What was the answer? And what was it, in the first place, that drove him to pray?)	(Two answers are given: the first about Jesus' destiny, the second about his identity.)

On reading the account you want to know not just that Jesus went up the mountain to pray, but how his prayer changed him. The interpretation of Jesus' prayer is given to us through the wonderful element. By the way the story is told, the evangelists are not just describing an event but are offering us the meaning of the experience; they speak not only about the experience of Jesus praying but reveal, through the vision and the voice, the significance of this prayer in his life.

The evangelists are interpreting the prayer experience of Jesus. "Moses and Elijah appear in glory" and they speak not only to Jesus but to us, the listeners and readers – so we attend to what they are saying. They announce something extraordinary: that Jesus' departure (*exodus*) is to be *accomplished* in Jerusalem. At the heart of this revelation is the truth that Jesus' departure, his final departure in death, will be the fulfilment of his mission, not its cancellation. His mission and his death are not contradictory forces; rather *Jesus' death will be the accomplishment of his mission.*

You can see this same dynamic – mission versus death – at work in the life and death of Archbishop Oscar Romero. He was repeatedly warned that if he continued to use his voice to support the oppressed people and oppose the military regime in El Salvador, he would surely pay the ultimate price. Romero had to make up his mind whether to stay in the country or organise his escape. He refused the invitation from the Vatican to take refuge in Rome and decided instead to remain with his own

² J. Dunn, *Jesus Remembered: Christianity in the Making*, Vol. I (Michigan: Eerdmans, 2003).

67

people and his own choices, knowing that staying on would mean certain death. By then he had developed a keen sense that his approaching death would be at the heart of his mission. Days before his murder Archbishop Romero told a reporter, "You can tell the people that if they succeed in killing me, that I forgive and bless those who do it. Hopefully, they will realise they are wasting their time. A bishop will die, but the Church of God, which is the people, will never perish."

Putting together a violent death and a fulfilled mission seems to be an unlikely reconciliation, but death does not have the last word. The mission will continue through death.

Luke tells us that the disciples have trouble staying awake and attending to what is happening. They see two men standing with Jesus, leading Peter to make the suggestion about building three booths. While Luke kindly explains that Peter doesn't know what he is saying, we see Peter opt for something, in the confusion, that he can manage to do: if you have no idea what is going on, build something.

God the Father doesn't think much of Peter's proposed architectural programme: we now hear the second revelation, "This is my Son, my Chosen; listen to him!" Building programmes are not what is needed; what is needed is to listen to the one whom God identifies as his Son, the Chosen One.

As the voice of Moses and Elijah focused on the *direction* of Jesus' life, so the Father's voice focuses on the *identity* of Jesus. These two voices indicate the answer to Jesus' prayer and also directly address the two conflicts he is facing.

The first conflict
How can his mission be accomplished when his death is being devised?
The answer
His journey to death in Jerusalem will be the fulfilment of his mission.

The second conflict
Given so many guesses about his identity, who is he?
The answer
By God's reckoning, he is the Son, the Chosen One of the Father.

In the clarity of these answers is it any wonder that Jesus' face changes, that he becomes radiant and aglow? In the prayer experience something shows through that was not showing through before; something is revealed that before this moment had never been disclosed. There is a strong hint that the prayer experience of Jesus helps him to take the road to Jerusalem – the difficult road that he knows will end with his own death. In the declared purpose of his mission and in the declared love of his Father the Chosen One will take the road to Jerusalem. In his prayer Jesus discovers an answer to his original question: "Who do you say that I am?" There is someone who knows his true name, and that someone is his loving Father.

After the voice speaks, the figures of Moses and Elijah disappear, leaving Jesus standing alone. In this dramatic tableau Jesus alone, not the great figures from the Old Testament, stands between heaven and earth. He alone will face the consequences of this revelation, that as Son and Chosen One he will take the road to Jerusalem, one that will eventually lead to another hilltop on Mount Golgotha, the place that specialises in disfiguring people to death. But again, disfiguration will not have the final word.

Against claiming too much

Jesus and the disciples leave the mountain top and come down into the valley – they must leave peak experiences behind them – to hear a father's scream imploring Jesus to look at his disfigured son. At the bottom of the mountain there is another son looking for transfiguration. The father says that he tried asking the disciples and they could not cast out the devil. The boy, suffering from acute epilepsy, moves towards Jesus. Jesus rebukes the unclean spirit and gives the boy back to his father. Another son is transfigured and restored.

Luke says that while everyone standing around is in admiration of what has been accomplished, Jesus says to his disciples, "Let these words sink into your ears: 'The Son of Man is going to be betrayed into human hands.' But they did not understand this saying; its meaning was concealed from them, so that they could not perceive it" (Luke 9:44-45).

The disciples do not understand what Jesus is saying, because the full understanding of who Jesus is and his destiny has been hidden from them. Luke stays consistent with his theological outlook that no one knows who Jesus is until after the resurrection, when the disciples will be clothed with the power from on high. Luke does not give us permission to interpret the transfiguration as a manifestation, a revelation of Jesus' true identity and destiny to his disciples, because when they get to the bottom of the mountain they don't know what he is talking about when he speaks of both.

All we know is that soon after, in Luke 9:51, Jesus leaves Galilee behind him and resolutely sets his face towards Jerusalem. We can make the connection between what happens to Jesus on the mountain and his decision to face Jerusalem. The Father doesn't just recognise Jesus but affirms him in love as his Son and Chosen One. That loving affirmation of his identity is allied to his destiny: being who he is means he must take the road to Jerusalem. And when Jesus comes down the mountain, that is what he does: he sets his face towards Jerusalem, where he will come face to face with the aching reality that his identity and destiny entail his death.

You can face the prospect of Jerusalem much better if you realise that there is a purpose to the violence you will undergo there, and that you are not making this journey alone but with the support of a

loving Father. Jesus will take this difficult road in that double belief.

Transfiguration in life
Bring the transfiguration into your own reflection:

> - What kind of suffering would you be willing to endure?
> - What purpose would make sense of your suffering?
> - For whom would you gladly suffer?
> - Who calls your name in love?
> - Whose name do you call in love?

We can call each other all sorts of names; we can relate to each other in all sorts of ways. We are lucky if we have family and friends who know us and love us, so that we move in the assurance that whatever we face in life, we do not face it alone and unloved.

One of the most telling things about Jesus is that transfiguration is not something that he receives exclusively for himself, but a power that he shares with legions of people. Throughout his public ministry Jesus transfigures many people – the broken, the wounded and the wayward. He calls to the deepest part of people and transfigures

Journey — Wilderness — Well — Mountain — Road — Table — Cross — Road

them by the power of God's love, the same power that transfigured Jesus himself. For Jesus the experience of transfiguration led him closer to his identity and destiny. And we all get closer to who we really are and what we must do when we hear our name called in love.

As the poet Philip Larkin wrote:

"In everyone there sleeps
A sense of life lived according to love –
To some it means the difference they could make
By loving others, but across most it sweeps
As all they might have done had they been loved."[3]

The power of being loved funds us to face the future, just as its absence makes the future a loveless landscape. In the transfiguration of Jesus, God demonstrated the depths of his love. It is that love that we celebrate. It helps us to travel hopefully; it enables us to keep on striving until we can rest at last in the love that knows our name best.

Summary

After questioning his disciples about who people say he is, Jesus takes his three favourite disciples up a mountain, to pray. During his prayer experience he is visibly changed. He is identified as the favoured Son of God, and hears that his mission will be accomplished in Jerusalem, even though that mission will involve his death. These two declarations resolve two challenges Jesus faces: (1) how people identify him; (2) his mission versus the likelihood of his death. Jesus comes down the mountain and sets his face resolutely for Jerusalem.

Prayer

Fill us, we pray, Lord, with your light and life
that we may show forth your wondrous glory.
Grant that your love may so fill our lives
that we may count
nothing too small to do for you,
nothing too much to give,
and nothing too hard to bear.
Through Christ, our Lord.
Amen.
St Ignatius of Loyola

[3] P. Larkin, *The Whitsun Weddings* (London: Faber & Faber, 1963), p. 15.

Mountain

Going beyond appearances

Transfiguration appears with regularity in the world of the Gospel and the world of the fairy tale – perhaps because of the recognition that, throughout life, disfiguration is such a common human affliction.

In fairy tales you meet people disfigured by evil curses imposed by others; you meet old hags whose innate kindness is rarely guessed at; you meet the youngest sons who have so little going for them but who end up as princes.

In the Gospel you meet a blind man who screams at Jesus, "Lord, have mercy!"; you meet a mad demoniac transformed into a quiet disciple who sits at the feet of Jesus; you meet a broken disciple transfigured by stubborn love.

In the fairy tale as in the Gospel, you should never judge by appearances: behind what appears to be ugliness there can be great beauty; behind what appears to be fragility, there can be great strength. Above all it is the power of love that transfigures. Think about the following story of transfiguration.

The Frog Prince
by the Brothers Grimm
One fine evening a young princess put on her bonnet and clogs, and went out to take a walk by herself in a wood; and when she came to a cool spring of water with a rose in the middle of it, she sat herself down to rest a while. Now she had a golden ball in her hand, which was her favourite plaything; and she was always tossing it up into the air, and catching it again as it fell.

After a time she threw it up so high that she missed catching it as it fell; and the ball bounded away, and rolled along on the ground, until at last it fell down into the spring. The princess looked into the spring after her ball, but it was very deep, so deep that she could not see the bottom of it. She began to cry, and said, "Alas! if I could only get my ball again, I would give all my fine clothes and jewels, and everything that I have in the world."

While she was speaking, a frog put its head out of the water, and said, "Princess, why do you weep so bitterly?"

"Alas!" said she, "what can you do for me, you nasty frog? My golden ball has fallen into the spring."

Journey · Wilderness · Well · Mountain · Road · Table · Cross · Road

The frog said, "I do not want your pearls, and jewels, and fine clothes; but if you will love me, and let me live with you and eat from off your golden plate, and sleep on your bed, I will bring you your ball again."

"What nonsense", thought the princess, "this silly frog is talking! He can never even get out of the spring to visit me, though he may be able to get my ball for me, and therefore I will tell him he shall have what he asks."

So she said to the frog, "Well, if you will bring me my ball, I will do all you ask."

Then the frog put his head down, and dived deep under the water; and after a little while he came up again, with the ball in his mouth, and threw it on the edge of the spring.

As soon as the young princess saw her ball, she ran to pick it up; and she was so overjoyed to have it in her hand again, that she never thought of the frog, but ran home with it as fast as she could.

The frog called after her, "Stay, princess, and take me with you as you said."

But she did not stop to hear a word.

The next day, just as the princess had sat down to dinner, she heard a strange noise – tap, tap – plash, plash – as if something was coming up the marble staircase, and soon afterwards there was a gentle knock at the door, and a little voice cried out and said:

"Open the door, my princess dear,
Open the door to thy true love here!
And mind the words that thou and I said
By the fountain cool,
in the greenwood shade."

Then the princess ran to the door and opened it, and there she saw the frog, whom she had quite forgotten. At this sight she was sadly frightened, and shutting the door as fast as she could came back to her seat.

The king, her father, seeing that something had frightened her, asked her what was the matter.

"There is a nasty frog," said she, "at the door, that lifted my ball for me out of the spring this morning. I told him that he should live with me here, thinking that he could never get out of the spring; but there he is at the door, and he wants to come in."

While she was speaking the frog knocked again at the door, and said:

"Open the door, my princess dear,
Open the door to thy true love here!
And mind the words that thou and I said
By the fountain cool,
in the greenwood shade."

Then the king said to the young princess, "As you have given your word you must keep it; so go and let him in."

She did so, and the frog hopped into the room, and then straight on – tap, tap – plash, plash – from the bottom of the room to the top, till he came up close to the table where the princess sat.

"Pray lift me up on the chair," said he to the princess, "and let me sit next to you."

As soon as she had done this, the frog said, "Put your plate nearer to me, that I may eat out of it."

This she did, and when he had eaten as much as he could, he said, "Now I am tired; carry me upstairs, and put me into your bed."

And the princess, though very unwilling, took him up in her hand, and put him upon the pillow of her own bed, where he slept all night long.

As soon as it was light the frog jumped up, hopped downstairs, and went out of the house.

"Now, then," thought the princess, "at last he is gone, and I shall be troubled with him no more."

But she was mistaken; for when night came again she heard the same tapping at the door; and the frog came once more, and said:

"Open the door, my princess dear,
Open the door to thy true love here!
And mind the words that thou and I said
By the fountain cool,
in the greenwood shade."

And when the princess opened the door the frog came in, and slept upon her pillow as before, till the morning broke. And the third night he did the same. But when the princess awoke on the following morning she was astonished to see, instead of the frog, a handsome prince, gazing on her with the most beautiful eyes she had ever seen and standing at the head of her bed.

He told her that he had been enchanted by a spiteful fairy, who had changed him into a frog; and that he had been fated so to abide till some princess should take him out of the spring, and let him eat from her plate, and sleep upon her bed for three nights.

"You", said the prince, "have broken this cruel charm, and now I have nothing to wish for but that you should go with me into my father's kingdom, where I will marry you, and love you as long as you live."

The young princess, you may be sure, was not long in saying "Yes" to all this; and as they spoke a brightly coloured coach drove up, with eight beautiful horses, decked with plumes of feathers and a golden harness; and behind the coach rode the prince's servant, faithful Heinrich, who had bewailed the misfortunes of his dear master during his enchantment so long and so bitterly, that his heart had well-nigh burst.

They then took leave of the king, and got into the coach with eight horses, and all set out, full of joy and merriment, for the prince's kingdom, which they reached safely; and there they lived happily a great many years.

Mountain

Questions for reflection

1. The experience of Jesus on the mountain top and the account of the Frog Prince are both told as stories of transfiguration. What do they have in common?

2. When you look around your neighbourhood, look further around the country, indeed have a look around our world: where do you see people suffering from disfiguration? Who or what do you think has the power to transfigure them?

3. If you had to face a very difficult and painful decision, what would enable you to face it? What would really help you face up to the challenges ahead?

4. What have been the "peak experiences" of your life? How long did they last? What purpose, if any, did they serve?

5. Do you believe that you have the capacity to transfigure people? If so, how do you see yourself doing this?

Final prayer and blessing

We pray for all those who feel defeated by life,
who believe that life has somehow passed them by;
we pray for all who are disfigured or scarred
in body, in mind, or in spirit;
for all those who are named and known
by their affliction or sin.

We pray for ourselves
that we might never undervalue
the power of love and attentiveness;
that we might never harbour our love needlessly,
nor ignore the little people in life
who hunger to be noticed and counted.

May the Lord look upon us
with kindness and mercy;
may the Lord shine his radiance upon us
and all whom we cherish;
may the Lord keep us for ever
in the embrace of his loving gaze.
Amen.

Along the road
Station Four

Along the road

The oldest story in the world

The oldest surviving story in the world is the story of Gilgamesh, the hero who leaves home and travels to the ends of the earth in search of the secret of everlasting life. Gilgamesh was a historical king of Uruk in Babylonia, in modern Iraq; he lived in about 2700 BC. Many myths were created about him, celebrating him as half-man and half-God, some of which were committed to writing around 2000 BC on clay tablets, which still survive. The fullest surviving version is from twelve stone tablets found in the ruins of the library of the king of Assyria from 669 to 633 BC, at ancient Nineveh.

The gods make a companion for Gilgamesh, someone who is also his opposite: Enkidu is half-man and half-beast, the original noble savage. Their relationship begins in a thumping fight, which moves into mutual appreciation of each other as true friends. Together the two heroes go to the Cedar Forest to kill the fierce monster Humbaba, which Gilgamesh succeeds in doing. Their challenges continue; their friendship deepens.

Enkidu falls mortally ill, and dies. Gilgamesh is inconsolable and proclaims:

"Hear me elders, hear me, young men, my beloved friend is dead, he is dead, my beloved brother is dead. I will mourn as long as I breathe, I will sob for him like a woman who has lost her only child."[1]

After the death of his beloved friend and travelling companion Enkidu – half-man and half-animal – Gilgamesh becomes profoundly depressed, not only out of grief for his friend, but because he now realises that he too, as half-man, must die. He decides that his new mission must be to possess eternal life, so he resolves to set out on the most perilous journey of all: to journey to the ends of the earth to meet with Utnapishtim and his wife, the only humans to whom the gods have granted eternal life. Utnapishtim was the great king of the world before the Flood; he and his wife were the only survivors whom the gods preserved. They dwell in the land of Far-Away, at the mouth of all rivers, on the very margin of the world.

After a long road and a perilous journey, Gilgamesh reaches close to his destination. Shiduri, the tavern keeper, gives him shelter and advises him to accept his human fate and enjoy life while he can. Gilgamesh

Journey | Wilderness | Well | Mountain | Road | Table | Cross | Road

insists, however, that he must find the two immortals, so the innkeeper tells him that the boatman Urshanabi can take him across the Sea of Death to the place where they live. Gilgamesh accepts the offer. When the two travelling companions reach the other side, Gilgamesh fails the test given him by Utnapishtim. He will never possess the gift of immortality.

Utnapishtim's wife convinces her husband to have mercy on Gilgamesh; in place of immortality, he offers Gilgamesh a secret plant that will make Gilgamesh young again. The plant is at the bottom of the ocean surrounding the land of Far-Away; Gilgamesh ties stones to his feet, sinks to the seabed and picks the magic plant. But he doesn't use it because he is unsure of its effect; instead, he decides to take it back to Uruk and test it out on an old man first, to make sure it works.

The ferryman Urshanabi becomes Gilgamesh's new friend and travelling companion, taking him across the Waters of Death. Several leagues inland, Gilgamesh and Urshanabi stop to eat and sleep. While they're sleeping, a snake slithers into their camp, eats the magic plant of eternal youthfulness, and crawls away. (This explains, dear reader, why snakes shed their skins!)

When Gilgamesh awakens to find the plant gone, he falls to his knees and weeps:

> "What shall I do now? All my hardships have been for nothing. O Urshanabi, was it for this that my hands have laboured, was it for this I gave my heart's blood?"[2]

What will Gilgamesh do now? His quest has failed, but he decides, humbly, to return to his people and tell them that they did once have this gift of life in their possession but lost it to a snake. At the end of the return journey Gilgamesh stands before the gates of Uruk, inviting Urshanabi to look around and view the greatness of this city, the true work of humanity.

The *Epic of Gilgamesh* touches people profoundly after so many centuries because it is about issues that connect with people, wherever they are: the search for direction and life; the beauty of companionship; the longing for immortality and perpetual youth; the experience of failure; the anguish of loss, and the inevitability of death for all human beings.

[1] S. Mitchell, *Gilgamesh: A New English Version* (London: Free Press, 2004), pp. 152-153.
[2] Mitchell, *Gilgamesh*, pp. 197-198.

Variations on a theme

The world of literature, including Homer's *Iliad* and *Odyssey* and Virgil's *Aeneid*, has been dominated by tales of heroic journeys, quests and conflicts, where the travelling hero is tested to the limits of his strength.

You can see the same theme repeated in the cycle of J.R.R. Tolkien's *The Lord of the Rings*. The hero faces dangerous places and must endure a litany of trials; he must also come to terms with his own inner demons and summon the necessary strength and willpower to see through his original mission. The way he handles conflict and trial will win or lose the admiration of the reader/viewer.

The image of life as a journey of discovery, without and within, continues today in its clearest form in "road movies" – for example:

- Easy Rider
- Alice Doesn't Live Here Anymore
- Rain Man
- Wild at Heart
- Thelma and Louise
- The Motorcycle Diaries.

All the characters share an edgy dissatisfaction about staying where they are, believing that redemption will be found on the road – somewhere. In his article "The Road Movie", Sam North writes that this type of film, a variation of the ancient quest story, traditionally ends in one of four ways:

- having met with triumph at their ultimate destination, the protagonist(s) return home, wiser for their experiences
- at the end of the journey, the protagonist(s) find a new home at their destination
- the journey continues endlessly
- having realised that, as a result of their journey, they can never go home, the protagonists either choose death or are killed.[3]

Journey — Wilderness — Well — Mountain — Road — Table — Cross — Road

In terms of the movement of the Gospel story, the Jesus story could be filmed as a road movie. The road to Jerusalem dominates the narrative, and the ministry of Jesus is told through a journey from the highlands of Galilee in the north to the southern city of Jerusalem, the place where the country prophet will come to a violent end. Jesus leaves home and returns only once – to experience rejection by and hostility from his own townspeople and relatives. When he escapes from home after being spurned, he never returns but heads away, steadfastly remaining as an independent wandering teacher and healer, on the road, for the remainder of his ministry.

That road ends when he is killed by the authority figures in the city of his destination.

When Jesus speaks of himself as the wandering shepherd he is clearly allying himself with the vagabonds of society, the outsiders, those who survive outside human habitation, on the fringes of society. In describing his own way of living Jesus says: "Foxes have holes, and birds of the air have nests; but the Son of Man has nowhere to lay his head" (Luke 9:58).

He is the itinerant prophet who has been rejected by his own people in Nazareth. He keeps moving, always having another address in mind, and in the course of his ministry he shakes a lot of dust from his feet. He never lingers in one place – even when the locals' hospitality is generous and they want him to settle down as their resident town healer. He will not be tied down – except when he is taken and led out to Golgotha.

3 S. North, "The Road Movie", *Hack Writers* [online magazine] (2007): <http://www.hackwriters.com/roadone.htm>.

Road

Gospel text: Luke 9:51-56; 10:1-6

When the days drew near for him to be taken up, he set his face to go to Jerusalem. And he sent messengers ahead of him. On their way they entered a village of the Samaritans to make ready for him; but they did not receive him, because his face was set towards Jerusalem. When his disciples James and John saw it, they said, "Lord, do you want us to command fire to come down from heaven and consume them?" But he turned and rebuked them. Then they went on to another village…

After this the Lord appointed seventy others and sent them on ahead of him in pairs to every town and place where he himself intended to go. He said to them, "The harvest is plentiful, but the labourers are few; therefore ask the Lord of the harvest to send out labourers into his harvest. Go on your way. See, I am sending you out like lambs into the midst of wolves. Carry no purse, no bag, no sandals; and greet no one on the road. Whatever house you enter, first say, 'Peace to this house!' And if anyone is there who shares in peace, your peace will rest on that person; but if not, it will return to you."

Road

Reflecting on the Gospel story

Jesus leaves all behind him – home, family, neighbours, work – and takes to the road. He says goodbye to everything familiar to him, leaving it all over his shoulder. From a settled life in the small village of Nazareth, he becomes a pioneer, not only in taking new roads and gathering new friends and devising new means of reaching out to people on the way, but also in attracting a formidable cluster of new enemies. The transition from the quiet, settled life of a village carpenter to becoming a wandering teacher must have been a particularly challenging one: you have to say goodbye to the small world of the secure and familiar, turn around, and face a larger world of insecurity and strangeness.

The famous lines of Robert Frost from "The Road Not Taken" are appropriate:

"I shall be telling this with a sigh
Somewhere ages and ages hence:
Two roads diverged in a wood, and I –
I took the one less travelled by,
And that has made all the difference."[4]

Gathering companions for the road ahead
In the Gospel story, the evangelists present Jesus as a man who can command loyalty and respect and devotion; he has the capacity

to attract disciples to leave their homes and jobs and families to follow him on the road. Clearly he makes an impact on people, and because of this positive impression people become interested in who he is and in his mission.

The impact happens first; the interest comes second. Without the initial impact there would be no interest: we don't become interested in people who make no impact on us. If Jesus had done and said the same as all the other rabbis, no one would have asked the question: "Who is this man?" That question presupposes that Jesus has made a significant impact, provoking people to wonder about his identity.

Because of Jesus' verbs, because of what he makes happen, people begin to wonder who the subject of the verb is. Impact leads to wonder: the impact of the verb leads people to wonder about the identity of the person who has done this particular thing.

- *Who is this man that he even forgives sins?*
- *Who is this man who commands the waves to be still?*
- *Who is this man who opens the eyes of the blind?*
- *Who is this man who heals on the sabbath?*

Journey · Wilderness · Well · Mountain · Road · Table · Cross · Road

None of the disciples would have followed Jesus if they had not been first attracted by him and the power of his message. You do not give up everything to follow someone who looks primed for failure, someone who appears to be heading nowhere. On what basis would you leave everything to follow someone? Who would that person have to be and what would they have to do before you would attach your life to theirs?

Permit me to diverge, dear reader, for a moment. As a youngster I remember seeing an advertisement on television that strangely appealed to me. A man walks alone down a deserted street in a run-down part of the city. It is night-time. Tall vacant buildings appear behind him; there is no sign of life anywhere except, from somewhere in the background, you hear a dog barking. It is raining heavily. The man's wide-brimmed hat does not appear to be protecting him from the pouring rain. He pulls his wet coat collar around his neck and stops under the only lamp post in the street. He takes out a packet of cigarettes, lights one and breathes out a whiff of smoke. A voice-over declares: "You are never alone with a Strand." End.

Strand cigarettes died a quick market death – not, I presume, because they

were tasteless to cigarette smokers, but because so few people bought them owing to the miserable association projected by this advertisement. The forty-second advertisement proved memorable for many people, but few smokers wanted to buy Strand cigarettes and associate themselves with a lonely man, in abject surroundings, on a wet night, whose only comfort in life seemed to be a cigarette. Who would want to follow him?

Who would want to take out a packet of Strand cigarettes in company and have others associate them with this lonely figure who looked like he had nowhere to go?

[4] R. Frost, "The Road Not Taken", in G.W. Allen, W.B. Rideout and J.K. Robinson (eds), *American Poetry* (New York: Harper & Row, 1965), p. 668.

People don't associate naturally with what they perceive to be failure or desperation. To give up the life you have known, and take a new road, you need to believe that the person calling you and the new way of life offered both hold out new prospects and new challenges. Why else would you change? It is a measure of Jesus' natural authority, to say nothing of the attractiveness of his personality, that he could call others to a new way of life. They must have seen in him a new way of being in the world, a new road to walk. He became the new way.

Setting your face for the road

Jesus first ministers in his own region of Galilee, which, geographically, appears to be a safe distance from the religious authorities in Jerusalem. Luke tells us that Jesus "set his face" to take the road to Jerusalem. If you have to set your face to go to a particular place, it suggests that you would rather stay where you are or head for somewhere else. W.C. Fields famously proposed as his epitaph: "On the whole, I'd rather be in Philadelphia." Setting your face towards a place implies difficulty, if not danger, on the road ahead; it suggests that resolute determination will be needed. This journey will be neither easy nor agreeable, but will require sacrifice. For sure.

Jesus and the disciples begin their journey south by travelling through Samaria, and they are met with open hostility, giving them a taste of things to come. The Samaritans reject them – probably because they believe that this group is travelling to a theological mistake in the city of Jerusalem. The antagonism was mutual between the Jews and the Samaritans, illustrated by the response of two disciples. What do you do when people reject you? What do you do when you put on your best face, smile your most engaging smile, and all you get in return is sullen indifference and condemnation?

Two of the disciples, James and John – who, unsurprisingly, have earned the nickname "sons of thunder" because of their thumping temper – make an interesting pastoral suggestion to Jesus: call down fire from heaven and burn these people up.

Their inclination is to organise a holocaust and turn their enemies into ashes. While not a civilised proposition, it reflects how many people feel when they are hurt: they want to hurt the others more, diminish them, even annihilate them. Make people suffer like I am hurting: make them pay for how I feel.

The disciples appeal to raw power for the purpose of dominating others – an appeal that Jesus has already dismissed in the wilderness when Satan offered him immediate sovereignty over the kingdoms of the world. The appeal now comes from two of his own disciples, not from Satan.

Jesus rebukes them and then does himself what he will often counsel his disciples to do: if people reject you, shake the dust from your feet and move on. Move on! Do not become captivated by others' meanness of spirit or their miserable and miserly ways; otherwise you will end up building a monument to your own rejection, and spend the rest of your life telling the story. Move on and keep going until you meet people kind enough to make you welcome. This will make the disciples dependent on the kindness of strangers.

In this passage you see that Jesus' disciples do not come to him with empty heads, but join the group with a store of psychological baggage. The disciples bring into their relationship with Jesus and into their relationship with each other not only their real commitment and enthusiasm, but also:

- their own prejudices
- their unresolved compulsions
- their inability to handle rejection
- their sleeping violence
- their unformed theology
- their ready anger
- their jealousy at others' success
- their collected guilt
- their strange in-laws
- their suspicions
- their lust for greatness
- their misinformation about people
- their own unhealed hurts
- their thin resolve when things get tough
- their embarrassment and fear when Jesus is taken from them.

Jesus has a lot of work to do during this journey to evangelise his own crowd, never mind any other crowd. As Jesus journeys through different places and spaces, he wants to give his disciples not only a direction but also a perspective. The journey is not just from one place to the next but from one perspective to the next. He wants them to borrow his eyes, to see, ever so gradually, people and the world differently, more kindly. It is not just the road that they travel together; it is his viewpoint that they are invited to share.

Following the way of the master

Whatever disposition his followers have, Jesus needs their help. He is not a perfectionist, aggressively demanding that his disciples measure up to his ideals before risking them on the road, afraid that they will not shine in the task ahead. After all, Jesus has only one voice, one pair of hands: he needs his disciples if his message is to spread beyond the reaches of Galilee. One of Jesus' wonderful attributes is that he trusts his disciples in all their fragility, sending them out ahead of him. "Go on your way," he commands them – a command that, in the circumstances, seems either incredibly hopeful or utterly foolhardy.

If some of us were training the disciples, I fear they would probably be still in formation, awaiting our critical approval! After so short a training, Jesus sends them out on their own, to find their own roads, hoping that, in spite of all their vulnerability, their love and commitment might be caught by others who meet them. He hopes that the love they have for one another – not their efficiency – might be catching; it might intrigue people to become interested in the project.

Compared to the strength of his opponents, Jesus is aware that his own disciples are like lambs among wolves: in other words, they must be prepared to be eaten alive. Such is the urgency of preaching the kingdom that Jesus takes this epic risk: time, after all, is not on his side.

In other words the disciples are not just to follow Jesus but to make their own roads in life. The disciple is challenged to become like the master, to share his power.

The master will not be around for ever; the disciple will have to take over and become a leader and attract other people to the movement. Disciples must not only follow but become new leaders in their own turn. Above all, they must grow into their own authority, one that reflects the gentleness and attentiveness of Jesus himself.

There is a wonderful story, I think from India, which illustrates the nature of real discipleship. It goes something like this:

Journey · Wilderness · Well · Mountain · Road · Table · Cross · Road

Once upon a time a poor man was visited in his dream by the Lord Shiva who commanded him to wake early in the morning, walk to the edge of the village, and there to find a sleeping guru. He must wake the guru and tell him that the Lord Shiva had commanded that he give the poor man the gift of the largest diamond in the world.

The poor man was so excited that he didn't sleep for the rest of the night and was restless when dawn announced itself. He hurried to the edge of the village and saw, under a hedge, an old man asleep. "Guru, guru," he called. No answer. He bent down beside the old man and shook him awake. "What is it you want?" the guru asked.

The poor man replied that the Lord Shiva had commanded him to tell the guru to give him the largest diamond in the world. The guru said, "Oh, that thing; just wait a moment." He rose from his slumber, disappeared behind a great rock, and then emerged with a huge sack from which he extracted the most brilliant cut diamond in the world. "Here it is," the guru said, "take it and go your way in peace."

The poor man thanked him and ran back to his hut where he placed the diamond carefully under his bed. When he lay down that night the brilliance of the diamond shone in the dark. The poor man could not sleep but kept thinking and thinking. Something was missing. Suddenly something struck him. The thought would not leave him.

Early next morning he took the diamond with him and returned to find the guru. When he awoke the guru for a second time, he returned the diamond to the puzzled teacher. He said to the guru: "Master, I am returning the diamond to you. There is only one thing I want from you. Teach me how to give away diamonds."

The poor man becomes a disciple because he wants to become like the master; he wants to share in the power of the master, not just receive the master's handouts, however lavish. The question is: will the master share his power or will he keep his disciple as a slave, forever dependent on him?

In his turn Jesus tells his own disciples: "I do not call you servants any longer, because the servant does not know what the master is doing; but I have called you friends, because I have made known to you everything that I have heard from my Father" (John 15:15). Jesus passes on everything to his disciples, so that they might find their own road in the world. That road, in time, they will have to walk without the master beside them.

The road

In the Gospel of Luke Jesus' journey on the road to Jerusalem, which begins at 9:51 and ends at 19:27 with the entry into Jerusalem, is an extraordinary travelogue which includes teaching on discipleship and prayer, healing sick people, exchanging bitter words with the religious authorities, warning people of hard times ahead, eating with rich people and poor people, and

watching people who would love to join his company walk away. You wonder if Jesus ever speculates how many of his followers will endure with him, right to the end. Will he be surprised that only the women make it to his final destination?

During the journey you watch how Jesus is challenged about his origins, his lack of formal education, his seriousness, his frivolity, his curious friends and his baffling choice of eating companions. His freedom and independence make many observers uneasy; they wonder by what authority he does what he does. He argues with his opponents, without exacting ultimate clarity from them; he does not snipe at them behind their backs, but confronts them and calls them names to their faces.

Whatever the drama is on the road, Jesus never allows the conversation to drift too far away from the challenges and suffering that await his company at journey's end. If Jesus had employed media consultants and spin doctors, they would certainly have advised him against his instinct to be real and open about what he saw around him and what he thought about life. His fearless speech would have terrified them: "Do you think that I have come to bring peace to the

earth? No, I tell you, but rather division!" (Luke 12:51). Most people would want to keep talk about suffering and division and rejection firmly off the agenda, but Jesus brings it to the forefront. He names what he sees, and he has a charism for provoking conflict. It's as if he says: "If they don't mention suffering, they're probably kidding you."

Jesus also speaks words of awesome tenderness to his companions on the road: he talks of their measureless worth in the eyes of God and why they should never underestimate the power of love within them; he tells them that no matter how lost and broken they might become, they will always be welcomed back to their Father's house; he assures them that their life of renunciation will not go unheeded but be rewarded many times over, in this life and the next. He has a hard time, however, getting his own crowd to believe in themselves and in their own aptitude for mission, but he persists right through to the Last Supper.

As they travel nearer and nearer to Jerusalem, the road gets shorter, the mood gets more solemn and the talk gets more serious. It makes you wonder: did Jesus ever feel like making a U-turn and hiking it back to the safety of the Galilean hills?

The end of the road: entering the city with style

Jesus' journey to Jerusalem ends when he organises his own parade into the city that is destined to kill him. It seems puzzling – not only to go voluntarily to the place where your innocence will not protect you, but to enter the arena of your own execution in the midst of song and acclamation. The commotion throws the city into turmoil as the people seek to discover: "Who is this man?" That question again. The city people are told that this is the prophet Jesus of Nazareth, from up north in Galilee. The northerner has come to question the south; the countryman has come to risk himself in the big city; the prophet has come to confront established authority. In spite of all the excitement and the hoots and the palm waving, it is deadly serious.

By the time the passion gets under way there is nothing to shout about. Processions that follow messiahs are triumphant affairs; processions that follow condemned criminals are timid by comparison, shabby affairs made up of those who bravely turn up and the legion of the curious, who can never be mistaken for disciples. After Jesus' arrest all of his male disciples will abandon him: one will betray him with a kiss; another will deny him with curses. Confronted with fight or flight, their fear will make the decision.

When the passion comes it brings with it a pressing question: can you still attach yourself to this man when all the authorities are ranged against him? Can you still believe in Jesus when the road he now walks leads to Golgotha?

Jesus himself presses on to the end of the road. When we speak of the passion of Jesus we usually mean the suffering and death inflicted on him. But the passion is not just something that is done to Jesus by others; it is a power within Jesus, his passion that enables him to face the violence and the pain. Jesus has a grand passion, one that consumes his whole person and drives him through this time of horror. He could have avoided coming south to Jerusalem; he could have compromised and settled for survival. But the passion that is in him is grander than his need for security or survival. He is a deeply passionate man. His ardent love insists that he face the ultimate test of love – the cross.

Throughout his journey Jesus has revealed the reaches of his own passion. His undying urge to do his Father's will. His preference for the poor and the abandoned. His fury at a religious authority that exacts inflexible standards, crushing the broken reeds, all the while inventing new burdens for people to carry. His energetic love for those who are disabled in life, for those who have been unlucky, for those who are stuck in wretched ways, for prisoners who never hear good news. His open disappointment with those who are economical with their love, reserving the lion's share for themselves. His way of having basketfuls of plenty, pressed down yet still spilling over. His outlandish attachment to those who count themselves worthless. His dogged loyalty to those who will abandon him.

None of this emerges from a man who is faint-hearted or stingy in his ways; it reveals a man who relishes people, particularly the countless number of those who are lost – a man of grand passion. In the end the cross comes as no surprise: it is the penalty for making a habit of such extravagant love.

Summary

As a wandering prophet and wayfarer, Jesus spends his public ministry wending his way through towns and villages, never settling anywhere, staying on the road until journey's end. He does not travel alone but is accompanied by a band of disciples, men and women: the road becomes their classroom for teaching. Only the women will follow him on the final part of his journey, the Via Dolorosa. Jesus' long journey to Jerusalem is a time for teaching and healing, and for telling stories; it is a time for deepening friendships and for confronting enemies; it is a time to stay focused on his mission until his journey is completed in his death.

Prayer

In thy journeys to and fro
God direct thee;
in thy happiness and pleasure
God bless thee;
in care, anxiety or trouble
God sustain thee;
in peril and in danger
God protect thee.

The Church in Nigeria

Road

Pioneers and settlers

When I was a kid, Saturday afternoons were usually dedicated to going to the pictures, as we called them in Scotland, and the usual diet of films leaned towards Westerns. We were drawn into a world of limitless horizons, constant movement through unmapped landscapes, cowboys, horses, wagon trains, Indians, and, of course, endless conflict and fighting. The four of us – two eager brothers and two dutiful sisters who tagged along – clutching our ninepence each, would saunter over to the grandly named cinema, La Scala, which was owned by a wee Scots-Italian who dreamed he was still in Milan rather than in Clydebank.

During these films there was little ambiguity about the characters: there were the good guys and the bad guys. The hero was always a wholesome-looking fellow with a wholesome-looking horse. He usually wore a large white hat and had a pearl-handled revolver. Both hero and horse had good teeth and breathed sincerity, although sometimes the horse looked more intelligent than the hero. The villain, on the other hand, was dressed down to his spurs in black. He was always unshaven, looked allergic to soap, and his moustache and teeth were, predictably, black.

Most of the characters in the films fitted into two categories: the pioneers and the settlers. The pioneers were those who never liked being tied down, who hankered after new faces and new frontiers, who were happy answering the call of the wide, open spaces. Heading west, the pioneers' home was usually a covered wagon and they left a litany of forwarding addresses in their wake. They always seemed to be moving on, anxious to be away. They regarded houses as wallpapered traps which were more difficult to break out of than break in to. Their hunger was for horizon, and their song was:

> "I was born under a wanderin' star...
> I never seen a sight
> that didn't look better looking back."[5]

In contrast, there were the settlers. As the pioneers longed for freedom, the settlers longed for security. They had stopped wandering and now had established themselves at regular addresses; their wagons now stood idle, decorative souvenirs of a former life. They had put down roots, built their homes, raised a family, and surrounded themselves with familiar faces and extensive fences. They liked the settled life and the security that

Journey — Wilderness — Well — Mountain — Road — Table — Cross — Road

went with it. They had arrived and lost their hunger for elsewhere. When they had to leave home, they would never stay away too long. Instinctively suspicious of foreign places and foreign food and foreign people, they would guard their homesteads with their lives from intruders. And usually all the authority figures – the mayor, the sheriff and the judge – were settlers.

You will remember that the first two brothers in the Bible, Cain and Abel, are a settler and a pioneer. Abel is the shepherd, the wandering figure who searches out new pastures for his flock. Cain is the one who is settled, the farmer who tills the soil and waits on the produce from the land. Although they are brothers, the shepherd and the farmer, the pioneer and the settler, they don't relate very well. Cain is jealous because the sacrifice of the shepherd is accepted by God while his is rejected. He takes Abel to the open country and murders him. Punished by God, Cain is doomed to be a fugitive, but he soon settles down again and becomes the builder of the first city. The settler has landed again.

The story of the first two brothers, the pioneer and the settler, acts as a summary of the history of the chosen people, the

people who moved from a nomadic lifestyle to a settled one. Their ancestor was Abraham, a wandering Aramean, and their story gradually shifted from wagon train to settlement, from movement to stability, from wide open spaces to towns and villages. Their dream was not to stay free on the road but to settle down in the Promised Land. And when they eventually came into land, they carefully divided it among the twelve tribes of Israel. The people who began as refugees and itinerants, wandering with their animals in the desert, eventually moved into real estate and focused on tilling the soil. The settler won out. That radical change would be reflected in how they thought of God.

Jesus, the wayfarer

Long before the chosen people settled into the Promised Land, they were a nomadic people, fugitives, transients, wandering from place to place. They lived in tents and they led their animals from one pastureland to another. God travelled with them in the Ark of the Covenant – unsurprisingly on wheels. But when they came into the land, their sense of security shifted from being a travelling people to being a landed people. They even built God a house, a grand residence in the temple – so that, like them, God would now have one address. If they were landed, so God should be.

At the time of Jesus, the shepherd, the natural nomadic, was still an important worker, but was not looked on with great confidence. The old rivalry between the nomads roaming with their flocks and the settled workers of the land was still alive. Shepherds were regarded as an unhappy mixture of gypsy and roaming thief, not least because their flocks sometimes ate their way through private property.

Because of the roving nature of their job they couldn't honour the demands of the ceremonial law and so were regarded as religious outcasts; and because they were seen as untrustworthy, they were disqualified from appearing as legal witnesses.

The popular, romantic image of the shepherd that many of us have is a world away from the reality of the Gospels. It does not include living on the fringes of civilisation, the harshness and danger of the wilderness and wild animals, the smell of the unwashed, the expansive loneliness and the sheer difference of a life that communes more with sheep than with people.

The shepherd had a place in the folklore of the Israelite people but had no place of importance in their society at the time of Jesus. For a landed people, the shepherd reminded them of their insecure past: the shepherd was other than they were now. The psalm "The Lord is my shepherd" was now off the charts.

Seeing himself as a shepherd among landed people, Jesus would, in our understanding, be a counter-cultural figure. His chosen image would be calculated to upset the people who wanted to forget their troubled past and focus on their secure arrival into property. Jesus sees himself as

Journey — Wilderness — Well — Mountain — Road — Table — Cross — Road

going ahead of his flock seeking out new pastures. He takes on the risks and dangers of the calling, knowing that there will be a few wolves on the uplands. The authority figures – all settlers – regard him with undisguised suspicion, even hatred. They will eventually ensure that he is taken into the killing fields and murdered. They will tie him down at last. But he does not settle into death, and the tomb is a temporary stop. Clearly, you cannot keep *this* pioneer down.

A church of pioneers and settlers

When you think about yourself, dear reader, do you see yourself as a pioneer or a settler? Which is more important to you: freedom or security? Horizon or homestead? Do you want to map out new ways or are you happy staying put where you are?

Is the Church made up of both kinds of people? Think of the apostle Paul: a tentmaker who spent his life travelling around as a preacher. Think of the apostle James, the head of the Church in Jerusalem and the brother of the Lord, who stayed around to build up the local community. The apostles Paul and James did not get on particularly well – no surprise there. But every community needs both kinds: people who call the community away from stagnation, and people who build up the community.

We pray that the Church will attract people of a pioneering spirit, who will carry the word to distant places and cultures, missionaries who will map out new ways of being church and will stay alert to the times we live in. We pray that the Church will also attract settlers, people who will be there for others, who will stay around to build up the local community, and care for it in the Lord's name.

Road

Questions for reflection

1. When we meet most people, we are like ships that pass in the night. Have you met anyone in your life who has gifted you with a new way of looking at people and looking at the world?

2. Why do you think Jesus chose to take the road to Jerusalem, knowing that the road would end with an appointment with death?

3. What roads have you chosen in life that have determined who you are today, that have "made all the difference"? Looking back, what roads do you now regret taking?

4. If life is a journey from the womb to the tomb, how far along life's road do you think you are now? What is still outstanding on your life's agenda? What is left undone? What are you hoping will happen?

5. When you look back over the roads you have travelled and the people you have known, does your gratitude outweigh your regrets?

Final prayer and blessing

We pray for all who have had to quit home
because they were excluded and rejected;
for all who leave home as economic migrants,
unable to make a living where they first
belonged:
that the Lord will guide their steps
to new pastures,
to a place they can call home.

We pray for all who are fleeing from danger;
for all who are homeless and hungry.
We pray for them
and all who work to bring them relief:
that the Lord in his kindness
might watch over refugees and exiles;
those separated from their loved ones;
young people who are lost;
and those who have left or run away from
home.
We pray that they will arrive safely
at the place where they long to be.

We pray for all who welcome the stranger,
the itinerant, the outcast:
that they might know their generosity
is truly blessed by the God of all mercies,
who will, one day, welcome them
into the kingdom prepared for them
because they have ministered
to the hidden Christ in their midst.

God be with us on every road we take,
on every sea we cross,
through every sky we fly.
May the one who is Alpha and Omega
be with us
in our leaving and in our arriving,
in our rising and lying to rest,
in our dreams of the night,
and especially in our last hours on
earth.
Whoever we are,
wherever we might be,
may the Lord never withhold
his loving hands from us.
Amen.

At table

Station Five

At table
Profiling Jesus

Imagine you are an established reporter for *The Jerusalem Post* around AD 30. Your speciality is in interviewing visiting celebrities and local figures of interest. Apart from visiting scholars, few luminaries make their way to Judea – probably regarded by those who've even heard of it as a cheerless outpost – so your portfolio consists principally of profiles of influential worthies in the city and the surrounds.

Your editor was particularly pleased at the "Insight Profile" you did, in last month's colour supplement, of the Roman governor, Pontius Pilate, and his wife, Procula. While the pictures were lavish, the writing avoided being servile and could have been described as verging on the robust. That particular edition of the *Post* sold hundreds of extra copies. More importantly, the paper was not closed down.

Now the editor comes to your office and expresses his wish that you write an article on Jesus of Nazareth, the Galilean prophet who seems to have a curious charism for making enemies in high places. The editor suggests that you follow Jesus and his group for a few days, incognito, noting in detail what Jesus says, the different reactions he provokes, and observing the kind of people he seems at ease with and those he does not. Then you are to seek an interview with him. When your editor commissions you, he reminds you of the classic questions that must engage every reporter: Who? What? Where? When? Why? How?

He finally instructs you to find out in particular the answer to the questions: "What is Jesus' purpose, his mission? Who is he for? Who is he against?"

How do you think your article might turn out? In particular, how would you define the purpose of Jesus' ministry? What would you learn by watching how Jesus related to different people, by listening to his public discourses, by observing the way he handled conflict? As part of your profile, you always include a selection of other voices who share their impression of the main character: what kind of reactions might you gather from the people who met Jesus and his group of disciples? And if the best way of getting to know people is by relating to them, how would your own relationship with Jesus influence how you write about him?

Jesus' mission

Sadly, we have no portrait of Jesus that was written during the time of his public ministry; we have no articles, no interviews and no profiles. What we do have is a collection of narratives we call Gospels, which reflect back through the faith of the Church to the time of the original events. In the Gospels there is a fixed memory, now become a tradition, that Jesus reached out to a wide range of different people, particularly those who were beyond the boundaries of religious and social approval.

This movement to the margins of society was not incidental to his outreach but essential to his stated mission, which is summarily described in the Gospels of Matthew and Luke:

> "The Son of Man came to seek out and to save the lost."
> (Luke 19:10)

> "I was sent only to the lost sheep of the house of Israel."
> (Matthew 15:24)

Jesus' pastoral energies were focused on a group of people in his own society who are described as the lost – popularly identified in the Gospels as tax collectors and sinners. If those deemed lost are the focus of Jesus' interest and energy, how will he seek them out and minister to them? If you started a programme in your parish for reaching out to parishioners who had stopped attending the church, there would be little point in pinning a sign to the church noticeboard announcing a meeting for lapsed parishioners at three o'clock on Sunday afternoon. None of them would see it, since they don't attend the church. You would have to devise creative ways of reaching them beyond the confines of sacred space.

At the opening of the public ministry of Jesus a stage of conflict is set between sacred space and ordinary space, between the holy city of Jerusalem and the wilderness, between the priestly and the prophetic. If all the people in Judea and Jerusalem are going out into the wilderness to hear John the Baptist (Mark 1:5), the Gospel begins with a pilgrimage leaving sacred space and heading for everyday profane space. Normally pilgrimages head for sacred places or shrines; the Gospel opens with the reverse movement as people leave the holy city behind them, their destination being not a building but a person, the wild man and prophet, John the Baptist. In ministering in non-religious space, in the wilderness, John will attract groups of people that would never be spotted visiting sacred space: tax collectors, soldiers and prostitutes.

Jesus does not make his base in the wilderness, waiting for people to make their way to him; rather, he makes the decision to connect with people, taking the initiative in reaching out to them where they are. After all, if the focus of his mission is attending to lost people, they need someone to look for them, find them and invite them to a sense of being at home with God. But how to reach them?

Following John the Baptist, Jesus' ministry is based in ordinary space: although we catch glimpses of him ministering in the synagogue and the temple, the bulk of his time is spent in meeting people in open everyday space and in people's homes. Indeed, sacred space is seen to reject him. Unlike John's, Jesus' theatre of mission is considerably more expansive and varied: thus we see Jesus minister to people in the open air, on the seashore, on a hillside, in people's houses and also at table as he shares meals with a complex variety of fellow diners.

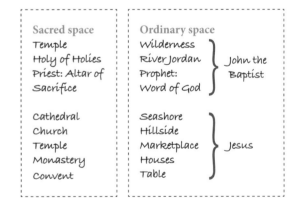

Sacred space	Ordinary space	
Temple	Wilderness	
Holy of Holies	River Jordan	John the
Priest: Altar of	Prophet:	Baptist
Sacrifice	Word of God	
Cathedral	Seashore	
Church	Hillside	
Temple	Marketplace	Jesus
Monastery	Houses	
Convent	Table	

├─Journey ─ Wilderness ── Well ── Mountain ── Road ── Table ── Cross ── Road

Jesus has an extraordinary facility to connect with people, and his pastoral strategy of associating with people puts him on a collision course with the Pharisees ("the separated ones") who stay carefully segregated from sinners. Their regular accusation against Jesus is that he welcomes and eats with sinners – appalled as they are at what they believe to be Jesus' haphazard and uncritical choice of table companions, which, they maintain, must surely render him unclean in the eyes of the Law.

If there is one practice that separates Jesus from both John the Baptist and the Pharisees, it is his open table fellowship, a distinguishing mark of his mission. He uses the table – an everyday place where people connect with one another – as the setting for revelation, for teaching and for grace-filled moments.

A telling example of this is when Jesus enters, at his own invitation, the house of Zacchaeus – an act that scandalises the ordinary people – and the house meeting moves the chief tax collector to make reparation for his way of life. Jesus happily proclaims: "Today salvation has come to this house… For the Son of Man came to seek out and to save the lost" (Luke 19:9-10).

As table fellowship was a distinguishing mark of Jesus' ministry, it is hardly surprising that he uses it as a summary of his person and mission at the Last Supper. On the night before he dies he gathers his disciples together at table, to share with them his most glorious gift: the gift of himself.

He will leave himself as food – not just food for thought, but real food – and hand over his complete self to them as a memorial. He will make himself a sacrifice to the God of all mercies. And he will leave them with the haunting request: "Do this in memory of me." Remember me by doing this; remember me by gathering in my name and breaking bread. When this happens, the memory lives.

Table

Gospel text: Luke 22:14-38

When the hour came, he took his place at the table, and the apostles with him. He said to them, "I have eagerly desired to eat this Passover with you before I suffer; for I tell you, I will not eat it until it is fulfilled in the kingdom of God." Then he took a cup, and after giving thanks he said, "Take this and divide it among yourselves; for I tell you that from now on I will not drink of the fruit of the vine until the kingdom of God comes." Then he took a loaf of bread, and when he had given thanks, he broke it and gave it to them, saying, "This is my body, which is given for you. Do this in remembrance of me." And he did the same with the cup after supper, saying, "This cup that is poured out for you is the new covenant in my blood. But see, the one who betrays me is with me, and his hand is on the table. For the Son of Man is going as it has been determined, but woe to that one by whom he is betrayed!" Then they began to ask one another, which one of them it could be who would do this.

A dispute also arose among them as to which one of them was to be regarded as the greatest. But he said to them, "The kings of the Gentiles lord it over them; and those in authority over them are called benefactors. But not so with you; rather

the greatest among you must become like the youngest, and the leader like one who serves. For who is greater, the one who is at the table or the one who serves? Is it not the one at the table? But I am among you as one who serves.

"You are those who have stood by me in my trials; and I confer on you, just as my Father has conferred on me, a kingdom, so that you may eat and drink at my table in my kingdom, and you will sit on thrones judging the twelve tribes of Israel.

"Simon, Simon, listen! Satan has demanded to sift all of you like wheat, but I have prayed for you that your own faith may not fail; and you, when once you have turned back, strengthen your brothers." And he said to him, "Lord, I am ready to go with you to prison and to death!" Jesus said, "I tell you, Peter, the cock will not crow this day, until you have denied three times that you know me."

He said to them, "When I sent you out without a purse, bag, or sandals, did you lack anything?" They said, "No, not a thing." He said to them, "But now, the one who has a purse must take it, and likewise a bag. And the one who has no sword must

sell his cloak and buy one. For I tell you, this scripture must be fulfilled in me, 'And he was counted among the lawless'; and indeed what is written about me is being fulfilled." They said, "Lord, look, here are two swords." He replied, "It is enough."

Table

Reflecting on the Gospel story

Throughout most of our lives we do thousands of things unthinkingly, ordinary routine things that we do every day with no great sense of drama or fuss. But we know that there will be a time in all our lives when it will be the last time, the very last time we do things. There will surely be:

- the last time we open the curtains to let in the morning light
- the last time we greet a new day
- the last time we speak to those we love
- the last time we hear our name called
- the last time we wonder if all the effort was worth it.

Perhaps it is a mercy that few of us are given to know when that last time will be. In Luke's scene of the Last Supper he portrays Jesus as someone who knows that the last times are upon him. At the opening of Jesus' ministry it looked like his death at the hands of the authorities might be a real possibility; then his death came to look likely if he continued his chosen ways; now, at the Last Supper, it looks inevitable, simply a matter of time – even of hours.

If you sensed that your death was approaching within hours – and you were still in good health – what would you do to prepare for your imminent death? If, for instance, you organised a final meal with a select few who were important in your life, whom would you invite? Why *those* people? And what would you say to them in your final hours? How would you like to be remembered by them? What would you want to leave behind you?

The Last Supper begins with Jesus sharing his earnest desire to eat this meal with his chosen disciples; it ends in frustration with the disciples displaying two swords and Jesus saying, "Enough of this." They leave the upper room and head for Gethsemane on the Mount of Olives, the garden of grief.

Sharing who you are
When Jesus gathered the twelve apostles in the upper room to celebrate their last meal before his death, one thing was obvious: it was not your usual evening out; not your usual celebration. When we look around at the assembled gathering we know there is treachery in the room, and it doesn't all belong to the company treasurer. There is awkwardness and confusion and hurt in the room; there is talk of betrayal and disowning; ambitions are exchanged about who is the greatest. That atmosphere of confusion and cross-talk is caught

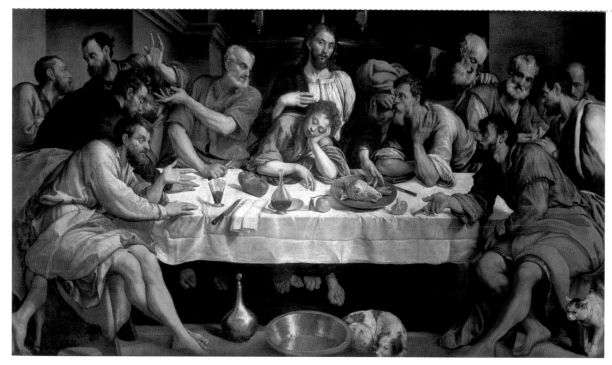

beautifully in Jacopo Bassano's painting *The Last Supper*. No one is attending to Jesus as he points out with one hand the head of a slaughtered lamb on a plate, and points to himself with the other hand. Is it any wonder that Jesus, as he looks out at us, the observers of this scene, concludes this meal with the exclamation, "Enough!"?

You can be in the same room with people, but on a different planet: proximity does not necessarily bring understanding. Sometimes when you try to be real with the people you know and love, they can turn away in awkward embarrassment, unsure how to react or what to say. They reach for anyone else or any topic – anything will do, apart from your revelation. Like the exchange I heard recently on the London Underground:

She says: "Have you any idea how that makes me feel? It really, really hurts."
He says: "Mmm. You know I got a promotion today at work. Cool."

At the Last Supper Jesus as host is talking about the brokenness of the bread and the bloodiness of the wine; his forthcoming death is fast approaching. At the table there is a noticeable absence of the lightness and fun we associate with celebrations. It is hard to be real with the people we know, but Jesus tries valiantly with his group. The apostles turn away from him as he struggles to say what is important to him, to have their own seminar about which of them is the greatest. A voice tries calling them back to a simpler vision of authority as service, which is so unlike the models in vogue around them in the Gentile world.

We talk of the celebration of the Last Supper. Why, if it was a celebration, did the host not go out onto the terrace overlooking the city and have a glass of wine with his friends? Why does he wander off into the night, walk through the graveyard of the Kidron Valley to an olive grove, to drink from a cup of grief – alone? Why does God ask him to hold up the world when he can hardly hold up his head? What is there to celebrate about the Last Supper?

If Jesus was only offering his disciples a share in his anguish and worries, then it would appear a very sad meal indeed. At the Last Supper Jesus summed up his own life – as people sometimes do before their death – as worthwhile. He had the capacity to see the difficulties without being overcome by them. He had the strength to look back at the halting progress of his ministry and see it all as worthwhile. Jesus accepted the fact that it was worthwhile to pay the price for who he was, a price that was exacted not only by his enemies but also by himself.

Because of the claims he made, because of the people he cherished, because of the values he professed, a bill was laid at his door. And he decided to pick up the bill. And the bill was himself, his own body and blood.

At the Last Supper we see the common struggles of community in the making. And just as the apostles were confused and uncertain about what was going on, that same drama can be repeated at our own Eucharists. But the good news is that Jesus can live with that. At the Last Supper Jesus broke bread for his broken community: he was breaking bread not for an assembly of heroes but for a fragile, confused group of followers. The Eucharist is always bread broken for broken people. Jesus keeps

telling us that our fragile humanity does not have to be denied or disguised to be accepted; rather in its fragility, in its shaky beauty, it is uplifted and transformed in the love of Christ.

The gift of Jesus is the gift of himself, *Corpus Christi*. And here we have the heart of the matter. Before Jesus is handed over into the hands of his enemies, he hands himself over, into the hands of his friends. He puts himself into their safekeeping, our safekeeping. This happens before the guards will come to drag him off into the night. He will be lifted up by the hands of his persecutors, but he will also be lifted up by the hands of his loving friends. And his body, *Corpus Christi*, will be in their safekeeping. And that will be throughout history.

That night before his death, Jesus said two haunting words: "Remember me." When I have gone, remember me; do this in memory of me. Eat the memory; feed off it. Remember my love. Remember it by doing it. This we do when we celebrate the Eucharist. But we hope for more: that we will not only be consumers of the bread of life but that we will become bread, one for another; that we will be a cup of salvation for one another. That is the best way to keep the memory of Jesus alive in our midst. We are charged to become the memory, to bring it into the present tense.

Jesus does not want his followers stupefied by loss, unable to move, to grow, or to advance life when he has gone. He wants them to cherish the memory of the time they shared with him, to feed off the good memories rather than be disabled by the sorrowful ones. He knows that they will divide their lives between the before and the after – the before when they were with him in Galilee and Judea and the after, when they have to live without his physical presence wherever they go.

Huge losses can divide life into before and after; they can become bold punctuation marks that stand out in our story. In the midst of loss it is very difficult to imagine what good can come from it all. Plans that seemed so exciting and important beforehand now look thin and insubstantial beside the weight of what has happened. Sometimes the loss can reduce us to silence, so we become dumb witnesses preoccupied with our own pain, unable to attend to the plight of others.

You notice how Jesus' friends are bewildered by all this talk. They will have to face the sudden death of the one they love and follow; they will be left behind, staring into a large absence. Their loss will affect the way they see themselves and their direction in life. An experience of profound loss always makes us question our own identity and direction in life. Who are we, as disciples, if the master is taken from us? What direction do we take when there is no one to follow, so that our very sense of direction seems to have gone?

Jesus encourages his disciples to believe in him; and if they continue to believe in him they will believe in themselves – as his followers. But first the disciples will have to face the time of dark, the loneliness of being left, the feeling of being abandoned when he is taken from them. What will help them in their struggle not to lose faith?

Before and after

There is a scene that has always helped me, from Ingmar Bergman's classic film *The Seventh Seal*. A crusading knight survives shipwreck on his return to his native land. His soul is sick with dread and longing. Needing faith, he hates his need for it; surrounded by corruption, he seeks a sign

that God exists. He wants to believe, but it is the time of plague, the Black Death.

The knight meets a peasant couple and their child on the road, and shares a meal with them. It is a meal as simple as a Eucharist: they only have wild strawberries – all the food they could gather – and fresh milk from a cow. But love is in the meeting place, in the touch and glance of the young couple, and love's fruit is there in their sleeping child. They even dare to play a song in the midst of plague.

And the knight is suddenly gifted with that meaning which is God's gift; the darkness leaves and he says:

"I shall remember this moment. The silence, the twilight, the bowl of strawberries and milk, your faces in the evening light. Mikael sleeping, Jof with his lyre. And I will carry this memory between my hands as if it were a bowl filled to the brim with fresh milk. And it will be an adequate sign – it will be enough for me."

"I shall remember this moment." At the Last Supper Jesus faces the darkness with nothing but his friends and faith in his Father. He hands himself over to his friends. We too remember that moment. We remember it each time we celebrate the Eucharist, when Jesus continues to hand himself over to us. We strengthen each other, break bread in his name, and feel a strength that is of God. The community has carried the memory carefully for two thousand years, and celebrated that meal in many forms.

Like the knight we can come to the Eucharist and be gentle for a while. We speak of God and take this food. And like the knight we can all say, "This will be enough for me."

Summary

Aware that his final time is approaching, Jesus carefully arranges a Last Supper with his chosen disciples. While he tries to use the occasion to share his thinking about his approaching death, his friends seem distracted, preferring to discuss which of them is the greatest. There is hurt and bewilderment and treachery in the room. In spite of that, and the fragility of the company, Jesus hands himself over to his friends, saying: "Do this in memory of me." This handing over continues in every Eucharist we celebrate.

Prayer

*Bring us, O Lord our God,
at our last awakening,
into the house and gate of heaven,
to enter into that gate and dwell in that house,
where there shall be no darkness or dazzling,
but one equal light;
no noise or silence,
but one equal music;
no fears or hopes,
but one equal possession;
no ends or beginnings,
but one equal eternity;
in the habitations of thy glory and dominion,
world without end.*

John Donne

Table

Jesus' body talk

When we reflect on the last hours of Jesus,
we think, among other things,
about what happens to Jesus' body.
It is a body that is taken, led away, handed over;
a body that is abused, tortured, stripped;
a body that is nailed down to lumber,
raised aloft in the Jerusalem killing fields
and exhibited as a spectacle for the curious.
It is a body thuggishly dismissed
to the anonymity of death.

But before Jesus is handed over to his enemies,
he hands himself over, with care, to his friends.
He takes the bread and solemnly says:
"Take and eat, this is my body, given for you."

It is a body given, pledged, bequeathed.
Jesus hands over his body –
not his ideas or his insights or his teachings –
as his final gift to his friends.
There is nothing more personal than this:
his own body is his lasting memorial.
What more could he give?

Sometimes, dear friends, we forget a simple truth:
that it was not only his body that Jesus left us as gift,
but it was through that same body
that he gifted people in his life –
through *Corpus Christi*.
The story of our salvation is told
through the body of Jesus.

Eyes

Think of the eyes of Jesus,
those eyes, educated by a magnanimous heart,
that looked out on the sweep of life
and appreciated such loveliness and majesty
where others glimpsed little or none.
Think not only of the word of God come among us
but of the eyes of God that graced the commonplace.

Jesus was not skilled at turning a blind eye
to awkward people or troublesome events.
His eyes were quick to notice so many small things –
like the widow at the treasury in the temple
who gave not out of her abundance
but from her poverty, everything she possessed.
She was left with nothing but Jesus' lavish wonder.

You watch as the rich young man comes to Jesus,
eager to join him, but then turns away with fallen face
from the unforeseen demands of discipleship.
And as he disappears back through the crowd
you watch Jesus steadfastly look after him in love.
The love that Jesus feels and offers, strangely,
is not dependent on the reciprocation of others.
His love is not a social contract,
but given without measure or calculation.

Finally, you watch the bruised eyes,
under a makeshift crown of thorns,
look down from the height of the cross
with forgiveness on those zealous for his death.
Then his sight dissolves with life itself.

Ears

Think of the ears of Jesus,
the ears that were assaulted by
so many screams for help:
"*Kyrie eleison*: O Lord, take pity upon me!"
Think of this man from Nazareth
who did not stop his ears
to people's howling and keening;
who never turned away from strident cries
that rudely interrupted his roadside seminars
with so many part-time students.
No, he was not the unmoved mover
of the philosophers,
but the one who was readily touched by the desperate
who yearned to reach the heart of God.

Think of the ears that were baffled and hurt
by the hostile cries of his own townspeople,
by the authorities' accusations, their scorn
and unsparing verdicts. The ears that heard
his principal disciple deny him lustily
to a little maidservant who opened doors in the dark.
At that point, we wonder,
could Jesus believe his ears?

The ears that, on the cross, could hear no more cries,
only his own inner howl at being stranded by God.

Touch

Think of Jesus' touch,
those hands that reached out and made contact
with a litany of people in gestures of comfort
and welcome and healing.
The hands that mixed spittle and clay,
pressing miracle into the eyes of the blind.
The arms that held up a little child as an icon
as he warned his disciples to leave off
being fascinated with themselves and hierarchy,
but learn to welcome the miniature people.

The hands that received people
rather than dismissing them;
the arms that held without crushing;
the hands that offered bread and wine
and awesome indiscriminate welcome.

Think of the arms that carried the weight of the cross
and needed help to endure the journey;
the hands that were now held back from people
because they were pierced and pinioned to the cross.
The hands that could no longer bear
the weight of his body, which slumped forward
into the collapse of death.

Nose

Think of Jesus' nose:
we don't know if it was big or small, wide or thin;
but we do know Jesus had a nose for
the marginal people in life,
the legion of the vulnerable and the broken.
This was the man who never looked down
his nose at anyone;
who never walked around with his nose in the air;
the one who could sniff out hypocrisy and corruption,
just as he could unearth hidden worth
in the strangest people.

We think of the one who breathed in
the fragrance of the lilies of the field,
and blessed God for the exquisite beauty of life.
We think of the one who had a delightful curiosity
about the world around him
and the people who inhabited it:
so he mixed with, and indeed ate with,
the crooked and the cracked,
the good and the bad, the virtuous and sinners,
thus becoming the most indiscriminate host in history.

He ended up having as his last companions in life
two crucified thieves –
retaining his reputation to the end.

Voice

Think of Jesus' voice,
a voice that spoke so many words
of tenderness and forgiveness to desolate people,
a voice that challenged and confronted
unyielding religious authorities.
This was not any voice but *vox Dei*,
whose message was so often lost on the wind.

His was the voice that protested against
the Pharisees and the scribes and the chief priests,
challenging them to abandon their hobby of inventing
newfangled burdens for people to carry.
They had become, he said, specialists
at smothering the wavering flame
and crushing the broken reed.

His was a voice that was forever mindful
of those whom life had subdued and defeated:
"Come to me all you who labour
and are overburdened
and I will give you rest."

The mouth that hymned the Beatitudes,
that begged, insisted we love one another
as he surely loves us,
is now given vinegar to drink.
The voice was silenced on Golgotha.

But not for ever.

⊢ Journey ─ Wilderness ─ Well ─ Mountain ─ Road ─ Table ─ Cross ─ Road

Feet
Think of the feet of Jesus,
feet that carried him to so many towns and villages;
feet weary and bruised from a nomadic way of life,
walking the rough roads of Galilee and Judea.
"Foxes have holes and the birds of the air have nests,
but the Son of Man has nowhere to lay his head."

These were the feet that trudged on and on,
without home to reach and rest.
But the feet carried a message,
as the prophet Isaiah proclaimed:
"How beautiful on the mountains
are the feet of those who bring good news,
who proclaim peace,
who bring good tidings,
who proclaim salvation,
who say to Zion, 'Your God reigns!'"

On the night before he died
Jesus aproned himself as a servant,
and sank to his knees
to wash the feet of his disciples.
Feet would make his finest homily.
If they missed the point of loving humble service,
of tender intimate devotion, of respect,
no Eucharist or ritual or extravagant liturgy
would ever compensate for that loss.

Liturgy, however grand, becomes suddenly irrelevant
when love is absent from the table.

If they missed that, they missed everything.
His own unwashed homeless feet
would eventually stagger and stumble
under the weight of a cross,
feet that would be spiked to an upright stake,
feet that, all too soon, could no longer buttress him
in life but simply give way in death.

Jesus' body
This was his body,
and through his body
came the grace of our Lord Jesus Christ.

It is through *our* bodies that
Jesus ministers to a broken world:
through our eyes; through our touch;
through our ears; through our voice.

We pray, in the words of St Augustine,
that when we gather for the Eucharist
we might become what we eat –
the body of Christ.

Table

Questions for reflection

1. You have twenty-four hours to live. About this there is no negotiation. It is fixed in the stars. What would you choose to do with the time left to you? Who would you invite, if anyone, to gather together to mark your final farewell? Or would you choose to make your exit alone? If you did gather a chosen group, who would they be? And what would you say to them?

2. When you look back over your own life, in all its ups and its downs, what would you like to leave behind you as a memorial of your life?

3. How is the confusion and hurt in the room of the Last Supper repeated today in our own churches? When you attend a Eucharist you bring with you your own worries and disappointments, your own dreams and hopes, and a bundle of distracted thoughts. You don't leave these in the church porch as you walk in to the assembly. On arrival the first hymn is: "Come as you are." Do you think the Eucharist can really embrace you as you are?

4. In what way can you be the body of Christ in your world today? If you think of tomorrow, what could you plan to do to make the memory of Jesus live through what you might do and say?

5. The Egyptian kings and queens were buried alongside a whole array of their favourite possessions and useful artefacts they might need in the next life, together with wheat, wine and meat, all in sealed containers. If you were allowed to take one thing with you into the afterlife, what would it be?

Journey — Wilderness — Well — Mountain — Road — Table — Cross — Road

Final prayer and blessing

We pray for all who are never invited to celebrations;
for those who are forever overlooked and bypassed
and who feel wholly unwanted.
That the Lord might open the eyes and enlighten the minds
of his disciples today to extend a welcome
that will give new life to the neglected.

For those whose hurt encloses them in isolation
because they cannot find words for their sorrow;
for those who are depressed in spirit
and disheartened and discouraged by life.
We pray that the Lord might lift them out of sadness
and reconnect them with the joy of living
and of belonging to warm-hearted friends.

We remember all who are approaching death
and facing their last times.
That they might know the closeness of family,
and the support and love of good friends,
so that they might depart this world in peace.

May the Lord of the living and the dead
look upon us with resolute kindness
and grant us the comfort of his peace.
When we are confused, may he bring insight;
when we are broken, may he mend us and mind us;
when we are dying, may he console us
with the assurance of his loving embrace.
This we ask in the name of the one
who gave everything of himself to us,
Jesus Christ, our Lord.
Amen.

On the cross

Station Six

On the cross

The passion of Jesus

In all four Gospels the evangelists head for the same place, the passion and death of Jesus, which is the longest narrative about Jesus in each Gospel. The writers develop the movement of their central drama through five scenes:

1. The arrest of Jesus
2. Jesus before the Jewish authority
3. Jesus before the Roman authority
4. The cross and death
5. The burial of the body.

All five scenes take place in a particular geography, within or around the city of Jerusalem, and it helps enormously in reading the passion story to get a sense of place for all this action.

The arrest of Jesus
Jesus is arrested by the temple police, at night, in an olive grove in Gethsemane, which faces across the Kidron Valley to the temple itself. The temple police were responsible for preserving order and making arrests on behalf of the Jewish religious authority.

Gethsemane is an image of sorrowful waiting, of being present to the prospect of what people will do to you; but it is also a story of resolve to endure, literally to hang in there. In the face of other people's pain, the temptation is to become apathetic. As my former professor, Dorothee Soelle, noted:

"Apathy is a form of the inability to suffer. It is understood as a social condition in which people avoid human relationships and contacts altogether... The desire to remain free from suffering, the retreat into apathy, can be a kind of fear of contact. One doesn't want to be touched, infected, defiled, drawn in. One remains aloof from people to the greatest possible extent, concerns himself only with his own projects, and isolates himself to the point of dull-wittedness."[1]

The story of Jesus' passion will go in the opposite direction: it will stay connected to people rather than remaining untouched; it will face the trial ahead rather than retreat into apathy; it will endure the pain rather than escape into avoidance. Gethsemane for Jesus is a crucial decision: he is going to wait it out. After being abandoned by his own disciples, Jesus is led away, alone, to the upper city, to the house of the high priest, Caiaphas, where there will be a preliminary hearing.

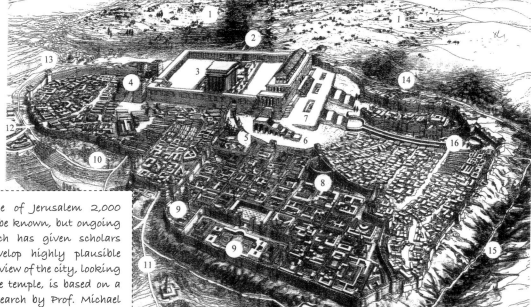

The exact appearance of Jerusalem 2,000 years ago will never be known, but ongoing archaeological research has given scholars enough data to develop highly plausible reconstructions. This view of the city, looking eastwards towards the temple, is based on a model built from research by Prof. Michael Avi-Yonah of the Hebrew University of Jerusalem. The map has been updated by the artist Nickie Jones, to include findings since 1968, following the Six Day War.

1. Mount of Olives
2. Gethsemane
3. The Temple
4. Antonia Fortress
5. Hasmonean Palace
6. Robinson's Arch
7. Ritual Baths
8. Theatre
9. Herod's Palace
10. Golgotha
11. Road to Bethlehem
12. Road to Galilee
13. Road to Jericho
14. Kidron Valley and Tombs
15. Hinnon Valley (Gehenna)
16. Pool of Siloam

Before the Jewish authority

Before going to Pilate the authorities would want to establish the guilt of their prisoner – not unlike the grand jury in the United States, or the role of the procurator fiscal in Scotland, both determining whether there is enough evidence for a case to go to trial. Popularly, these hearings, as in the Gospels, are often referred to as a trial.

Mark names the three groups that make up the Council. Firstly, the chief priests, including all the former high priests and those who held key leadership positions in the temple administration. Secondly, the elders, made up from the country's most prestigious lay families, the key landowning aristocrats (Joseph of Arimathea and Nicodemus would have belonged to this group). Thirdly, the scribes, the experts in the law; it was in this group that the Pharisees exercised their influence.

[1] D. Soelle, *Suffering* (Philadelphia: Fortress, 1975), pp. 36, 39.

The head of the council was Caiaphas. He remained in power from AD 18 to 37, a total of nineteen years. The average term of office for a high priest was four years, so it was a measure of Caiaphas' cunning and his diplomatic skills with the Roman authorities that he survived so long and outlasted Pontius Pilate.

In Mark's trial, witnesses for the prosecution are called: the testimony of these witnesses had to agree, otherwise they were regarded as worthless. No defence witnesses seem to have been called. The absence of defence witnesses has always intrigued me, since in Jewish law the prisoner had a right to call them.

Jesus is silent before the accusations of the witnesses, focusing on what he is alleged to have said about the temple, and their disagreement forces the intervention of Caiaphas. He asks Jesus: "Are you the Messiah, the Son of the Blessed One?" Mark has Jesus confess; Matthew has him say: "It is you who say I am."

Jesus is then mocked at the trial: bystanders strike him and challenge him to prophesy. There is a law of Moses against the false prophet: false prophets should be put to

death (Deuteronomy 13:1-5). But at the very moment they are mocking Jesus as a false prophet, Jesus' prophecy is being fulfilled down in the courtyard as Peter denies him.

Peter denies his own identity as a disciple and becomes a runaway. It is not just Peter's faith that is offered to us as Gospel, as Good News, it is also his failure. We hallow the memory of Peter's faith *and* failure; we hold holy the memory of his loyalty and disloyalty. Above all we remember that Jesus loved him throughout everything. Judas and Peter both betray Jesus, the only difference being that Peter comes back. Somewhere deep in Peter there is the belief that if he denies Jesus, Jesus will not deny him.

Before the Roman authority

First thing in the morning, Jesus is led away and handed over to the Roman authority – Pilate and his soldiers have arrived from Caesarea to preside over security during the approaching feast of the Passover. The Praetorium is the name of the judicial seat of the Roman procurator; it was established simply by hanging his shield on the gate and posting his tribune guard.

Journey — Wilderness · Well · Mountain · Road · Table · Cross · Road

Pilate's question, "Are you the King of the Jews?" suggests that the Jewish authority has presented the case under the aspect of Jesus as an agitator with political designs, a Christ-king in competition with Caesar himself. Thus we can understand why Jesus is crucified under the charge fixed to his cross: "The King of the Jews".

If the evangelist John is correct in his Gospel when he writes that the Jewish authorities observe, "We are not allowed to put anyone to death" (John 18:31), then they need the authority of Pilate to execute the death sentence over Jesus. If the Jews did have the right, Jesus would have been stoned to death, not crucified; crucifixion was especially characteristic of the Romans. The charge they make to Pilate is that Jesus is guilty of a capital crime punishable by death. But only the Roman procurator can make that decision.

Pilate is shown to believe in Jesus' innocence and offers to release Jesus as a festival favour. But the delegation for the release of a prisoner has already named their choice in Barabbas, who had been arrested for terrorist activity. Pilate would have regarded Barabbas as much more dangerous: it makes sense that he would try to use the release of Jesus to prevent Barabbas being released.

Pilate, however, underestimates the determination of the Jewish authorities to have Jesus brought to execution. According to John, the determining factor for Pilate's decision to execute Jesus was the charge: "If you release this man, you are no friend of the emperor. Everyone who claims to be a king sets himself against the emperor" (John 19:12). Pilate is shown as fundamentally insecure and wavering, a man who has reason to worry about his reputation with Tiberius Caesar.

To placate the crowd, the Roman governor hands over Jesus to be crucified. The Roman sentence was usually pronounced in three words: "Ibis in crucem" – you will ascend the cross.

The cross and death
After being mocked by the soldiers, Jesus is led away to the place of crucifixion, just outside one of the west gates into the city. In the absence of any male companions, a stranger, from Cyrene in North Africa, is enlisted to help Jesus carry the crossbeam, the *patibulum*.

Probably Jesus was so weakened by the scourging that he was unable to support the weight of the crossbeam. The upright part of the cross, a stake, would already have been in place at the site of execution. Criminals carried, around their neck, the charge against them, the *titulus*; this was later posted above the cross so that everyone would know the charge against them.

Golgotha was a disused quarry, known as "The Place of the Skull". Jewish legend had it that the skull or body of Adam was buried there. On arrival the condemned would have been thrown on the ground and his outstretched arms would have been nailed to the crossbeam. The crossbeam and the body of the criminal were then raised, the crossbeam being fixed to the top of the stake.

Jesus hangs on the cross, under the title, "Jesus of Nazareth, King of the Jews". In the Gospels there is no focus on how Jesus looks or what he feels. The details of human interest have been excluded from the account. The details that are mentioned reflect the psalms, as if to say that what is happening is fulfilling the ancient plan of God.

Two others are crucified with Jesus, one on either side. The mockery is in the arrangement, for a king cannot appear in public without his council, and these two agitators are carefully positioned to the right and left of Jesus. (Only Luke has a good criminal.)

There are three different portraits of death: Jesus dies, feeling abandoned by God (Mark and Matthew); Jesus dies as he commends his spirit to God (Luke); Jesus dies seeing everything as accomplished (John).

The burial of Jesus
In the Roman world the penalty of crucifixion was worsened by the refusal of permission for the victim to be buried. The corpses of the crucified were further humiliated by being left on the cross until they were torn to pieces by birds of prey or wild dogs.

Crucifixion was so ghastly that the Romans reserved it for non-Romans, for those found guilty of treason or for slaves. The philosopher Cicero wrote, embarrassed that such a civilised nation as the Romans should have this form of execution: "A hangman, a covered head, and the very

word 'cross' should remain far not only from the body of Roman citizens, but also from their thoughts, their eyes, their ears" (*Pro Rabirio*, 16).

For the Jews the refusal to bury a body was to dishonour the dead; it also defiled the land. According to Deuteronomy 21:22-23: "When someone is convicted of a crime punishable by death and is executed, and you hang him on a tree, his corpse must not remain all night upon the tree; you shall bury him that same day, for anyone hung on a tree is under God's curse. You must not defile the land that the Lord your God is giving you for possession." So victims of crucifixion, according to the Law, were to be taken down and buried before sunset.

When John the Baptist died, he was buried by his own disciples. Jesus is buried not by his disciples but by a caring sympathiser, Joseph of Arimathea, assisted by the women followers of Jesus. The body of Jesus is lowered from the cross, wrapped in a shroud and laid nearby in one of the tombs in Golgotha rock. Jesus is buried in an abandoned quarry. The site will be noted by the women, for this place will mark the beginning of another story.

Cross

Gospel text: Mark 15:20-39

Then they led him out to crucify him. They compelled a passer-by, who was coming in from the country, to carry his cross; it was Simon of Cyrene, the father of Alexander and Rufus. Then they brought Jesus to the place called Golgotha (which means the place of a skull). And they offered him wine mixed with myrrh; but he did not take it. And they crucified him, and divided his clothes among them, casting lots to decide what each should take.

It was nine o'clock in the morning when they crucified him. The inscription of the charge against him read, "The King of the Jews." And with him they crucified two bandits, one on his right and one on his left. Those who passed by derided him, shaking their heads and saying, "Aha! You who would destroy the temple and build it in three days, save yourself, and come down from the cross!" In the same way the chief priests, along with the scribes, were also mocking him among themselves and saying, "He saved others; he cannot save himself. Let the Messiah, the King of Israel, come down from the cross now, so that we may see and believe." Those who were crucified with him also taunted him.

When it was noon, darkness came over the whole land until three in the afternoon. At three o'clock Jesus cried out with a loud voice, "Eloi, Eloi, lema sabachthani?" which means, "My God, my God, why have you forsaken me?" When some of the bystanders heard it, they said, "Listen, he is calling for Elijah." And someone ran, filled a sponge with sour wine, put it on a stick, and gave it to him to drink, saying, "Wait, let us see whether Elijah will come to take him down."

Then Jesus gave a loud cry and breathed his last. And the curtain of the temple was torn in two, from top to bottom. Now when the centurion, who stood facing him, saw that in this way he breathed his last, he said, "Truly this man was God's Son!"

Journey — Wilderness — Well — Mountain — Road — Table — Cross — Road

Cross

Reflecting on the Gospel story

For a moment, put yourself in Jesus' place during the time of the passion. Take a few minutes to allow the variety of images to speak to you and imagine how it might all feel.

- There is the mounting anger at your popularity
- You and your enemies snap at one other
- You watch as your own community begins to crack
- There is the final meal that ends in disarray
- Still, you insist, your own crowd are all worth it – really
- You are aware of deals being made behind your back
- Aware, too, that a disciple will soon be afflicted with amnesia
- You wonder why friends cannot stay awake to your pain
- You wonder why you have become such an embarrassment
- Lying on the ground, you beg God to get you out of all this mess
- There is a kiss that hurts more than a stab wound
- Being led away after leading, for so long, from the front
- The inane questions they ask you, as if your answers matter
- Being led away again – pass the football
- Knowing that your innocence won't make the slightest difference
- The waiting while others consult and talk about you
- Catching glimpses of normal life carrying on around you
- In the midst of your tragedy, there is business as usual
- Shopkeepers sell; shoppers buy; people rush home

- You are in torment; everyday life goes on
- Can you carry on?
- You watch as people turn away in disgust
- Who can attend the suffering of others?
- You are aware of the gathering of tourists at your crucifixion
- You know you are killer entertainment
- People scoff, safe in the knowledge you're tied down
- Chief priests howl in delight
- Soldiers yawn
- The women are silent
- You try to hold up your head
- You wonder what you did wrong
- How did you end up here?
- Could you have said things better?
- What did you miss?
- You don't move out of your hurt and disappointment
- You hear yourself breathing words of forgiveness
- Why make others pay for what you are enduring?
- The crown of thorns slips off
- There is no more time
- Suddenly
- You embrace the darkness like a friend
- It is finished – all so quickly.

There is nobility and dignity, yes, but it is not a scene of triumph – if you stay with it, inside it, feel it in your bones, without peeking ahead at the resurrection. It is an end-game. It certainly was for those who were there, for those who were left behind. Bereft.

There were no alleluias on Golgotha.

Yet, yet, yet: something is made manifest – as the poet Seamus Heaney observed, in this excerpt from his poem "Weighing In":

"And this is all the good tidings amount to:
This principle of bearing, bearing up
And bearing out, just having to

Balance the intolerable in others
Against our own, having to abide
Whatever we settled for and settled into

Against our better judgement. Passive
Suffering makes the world go round...

Prophesy who struck thee! When soldiers mocked
Blindfolded Jesus and he didn't strike back

They were neither shamed nor edified, although
Something was made manifest – the power
Of power not exercised, of hope inferred
By the powerless forever." [2]

"The power of power not exercised" summarises the beauty of this scene. In the wilderness Satan tempted Jesus with the kingdoms of the world, and Jesus refused the offer of such spectacular power, deciding to tread the ordinary road of powerlessness, a road that led him, inexorably, to the cross. He has to pay the bill for the *kind* of life he chose to live, for the *kind* of people he chose to stand beside, for his way of being human.

Did Jesus have to die on the cross?
Could Jesus have avoided the cross? Could he have made a detour around Golgotha and returned to the quiet district of Galilee? Could he have avoided execution and settled for a quiet existence by the shores of the northern lake? Did his way of being human demand the cross?

It was not Jesus who looked for the cross; it was others in authority that looked to the cross as a way to eliminate him. It was not the idea of the Father: God the Father is not a sadist who planned the destruction of his beloved Son. In letting go of his Son, the Father had to be vulnerable to what would happen to his Son at the hands of others. All parents take that risk when they let go of their children. God the Father, no less, did likewise. One of my wise teachers, the Jesuit George McCauley, put it strongly when he wrote:

"We cannot have the Father 'planning'
Jesus' death in any sense. If the Father
plans anything, it is that the Son share

[2] S. Heaney, *The Spirit Level* (London: Faber & Faber, 1996), p. 17.

in solidarity our human condition. But this means that the Son takes on the mystery of human freedom, or lack of it. It means that in acting, interacting, and being acted upon by others, the Son is surrounded by risk, coincidence, fate, windfall, surprise, accident, chance, chemistry, and chaos. These things are intrinsic to our human lives. Jesus gets caught like the rest of us in the middle of crisscrossing human freedoms.

He did not die, we must keep repeating to ourselves. He was killed, put to death, done in. His death was not something to be embraced with some subtle joy. To be unsheathed of our body in one tearing, terrifying wrench is an awful thing, no matter who it happens to be, no matter what sentiments accompany the event. His death, like ours, remains the stinking, grief-ridden, crushing thing that all death is. Let's try not to dignify it by having the Father plan it."[3]

Love did not demand the cross, but in the life of Jesus love ends up on the cross. *That is what actually happened.* That is, often, what continues to happen to self-forgetful love. Love chooses not to avoid the suffering that emerges from its

commitment. The avoidance of suffering is not love's governing passion; it cannot be.

Jesus could have avoided going to Jerusalem; he could have taken the advice of the disciples who warned him about the fate that would surely befall him there. But instead of avoiding Jerusalem, Jesus enters the city – publicly and loudly. He does not disguise himself and slip through a quiet gate; he heads a parade. And the parade ends up as another journey to the place of dying. This journey he endures to the end.

Jesus decides to confront the power that is set against him. And when he chooses to do that, like all people who confront oppression, *he makes suffering visible*. As Theodor Adorno noted:

"It is part of the mechanism of domination, to forbid recognition of the suffering it produces."[4]

The memory of Jesus is dominated by the cross, when Jesus was at his most vulnerable. It is by his wounds that we are healed – not by his cleverness or ability or power. By his wounds. We are healed not by the strength of Jesus but by his brokenness. That is why the cross, not the

tomb, has dominated as the iconic image associated with Jesus, one that has lasted down the centuries.

The sign of the cross
The cross of Jesus stands at the centre of the Christian story as the sign of the lengths love will go to in its passion for others. The cross is lifted up in the midst of the Christian community as a sign that someone thought we were worth all the pain and the suffering. The love of one who "did not cling to his equality with God but emptied himself" to become as we all are; and, as we are, to show us that in spite of our stupidities and madness, God loves us. All else is commentary.

Summary
As an exercise in putting yourself in Jesus' sandals in his final hours, it is a worthwhile exercise to meditate on the passion as if you were the central character and journey through the moments of the story. How does it feel to have all this happen to you? How does it feel to have all these people make decisions about you over which you have no control? As you watch Jesus choose to go through this time of terror, you realise that the love within him is stronger than any wish to survive. From the cross, it is love's wordless language that speaks to us.

Prayer
Blessed are you, O Lord almighty,
who illumine the day with the brightness of
the sun and delight the night with the glow of
fire, who has made us worthy to live through
this whole day
and come close to the reaches of the night.
Hear our prayers and those of all your people;
forgive us our sins, both deliberate and
indeliberate, and accept our petitions;
send down upon your inheritance
the riches of your mercy and compassion;
surround us with your holy angels;
cover us with the armour of your justice;
keep us in the ways of your goodness;
protect us with your power against any harm
or conspiracy of the devil;
grant us that this evening, and the
approaching night,
and all the days of our life,
may be perfect, holy, peaceful, without sin,
without stumbling or vain imagination;
through the intercession of the Mother of God
and of all the saints;
who ever pleased you since time began.
Amen.

From Evening Prayer, the Orthodox Liturgy

[3] G. McCauley, *The Unfinished Image* (New York: Sadlier, 1983), pp. 89-90.
[4] T. Adorno, *Minima Moralia* (London: NLB, 1974).

A view of the crucifixion: Pilate's wife

Imagine Pilate's wife, who in Matthew's Gospel is presented as sympathetic to Jesus, seeing the final moments of the passion from her window in Herod's Palace, which has a clear sight of Golgotha.

My husband, Pontius Pilate – I call him Ponty –
and I are in the Lookout Room of the Palace,
from where you can see over the city of Jerusalem.
You have noticed, I know, the cross
outside the window behind me, on Golgotha,
a disused quarry where criminals are executed.
The locals ran out of Jerusalem limestone,
but we have not run out of criminals,
so it's a useful place on which to stamp our authority.

Golgotha is outside the main western gate of the city,
a handy place to terminate those who scorn our laws
or unduly vex the authority –
in this case, my husband.
Everyone who enters or exits the western gate
has to pass by the exhibition gallery on Golgotha.
If you want to preside over a populace,
make sure your criminals are seen to suffer,
to terrify those who might follow in their wake.
There is no point in executing upstarts
on a green hill far away.

From the window I watch the sad theatre of the absurd.
Ponty sits in a corner,
not daring to look at his handiwork.

I watch Jesus stumble up the rock,
roped to the patibulum,
the crossbeam that his hands will be hammered to,
which will then be lifted up and placed securely
on top of the upright stake
before his feet are nailed together.
I see how the crossbeam has etched its own shape,
blue-red, into his shoulders.

I watch this king stagger like a drunken slave,
then keel over, smashing the rock blood-red,
before he is whipped to upright again.
He flounders, rises, spits dust,
lurches, manages the few paces left
before his journey's end is reached.
He falls down again, this time to greet the ground
like an old friend he has waited too long to see.
If I am not mistaken,
I see him kiss the rock he falls upon.

The soldiers cut the ropes with their swords;
then their hired carpenter moves in,
stretches Jesus' arms on the crossbeam
to attach flesh to wood,
and nail the body precisely according to instructions.
Jesus' body stretches and stiffens into line.
The sound of hammering echoes loudly
against the rocks.

Head down, Ponty covers his ears at this.

The ritual almost complete, the body is raised in place
and seated on a small wooden peg to bear the weight;
the hired carpenter now grasps Jesus' dangling feet,
lifts and couples them like two unlikely lovers,
presses them together,
bends them to the required angle,
pins them in place, then hammers the nail home
through protesting flesh into the stake.

That done, he stands back to admire
his crippling handiwork –
no need for adjustments, he reckons, textbook clean;
then, after wiping some blood from his face,
the carpenter packs his tools and makes for home,
another job well done.

Watching this, I notice for the first time
that there is no silence on Golgotha:
the street dogs yawn and growl impatiently,
crouching ready to attack torn oozing flesh –
this man they know can shoo nothing away.
Soldiers slap armour and joke about their last conquest;
the street vendors cry their bargain prices
of nibbles to the chattering tourists,
who linger to look, whisper to each other,
glad they have elsewhere to go.

Overhead the buzzards hover, their fury in check,
winging their incessant circles as they hold out
for that dead bulk and weight to give
before they dive to rend human rubble.

The demented women, always women, now look,
now look away, avoiding each other's eyes,
then draw their damp veils around their faces
to mop up useless tears for their lovers, family, friends.
They keep the habit of years,
turning up in dangerous places
to observe the brute theatre of male violence:
I watch them kill time,
waiting for the soldiers' permission
before they are allowed to move in
and pick up the pieces.

You watch as Jesus makes a painful shift
from being the one who healed the sick and the lame
to becoming the crippled one himself,
with neither interrupting angel nor healer in sight.
You watch this active man being propelled
into the passive voice:
from being the charismatic leader
who commanded his disciples, "Follow me",
to being the criminal condemned to be handed over,
whipped, scorned, led away, tied down, crucified.

You watch how Jesus is so quickly reduced
from being the one who made things happen
to the one who has to suffer what others do to him.
From being the guest who gifted jars of wedding wine
to the one who now slurps vinegar.
From being the leader who called out,
"Come to me all you who labour
and are overburdened and I will give you rest",

to being the desperado who now cries out,
"My God, why have you abandoned me?"

I absorb the details, alone at the window.
I see this Jesus, my husband's chosen victim,
hang naked, with nothing between him and his God.
I hear the chief priests shout their taunts,
sweet victory in every swollen phrase.
For a moment – was I dreaming? – I thought
the crucified Jesus looked up
at the Tower from his cross,
sought out the window where I stood
and held me, Pilate's wife, in his gaze,
his eyes drilling my soul.

I wonder, watching him hanging there,
his body's weight dragging against the nails,
if he is wondering what went wrong?
Does he review everything in his head –
all that has led to this place?
Could he have done things differently?
Could he have said things more clearly,
made his points more insistently?
Did he miss something along the way?
What makes people pick the sides they pick anyway?

Finally there is the time for no more thinking,
no more hurting, no more being.

The bruised eyes close;
the head collapses onto his chest;

the body pitches forwards, off the wooden peg;
the makeshift crown of thorns loses its grip and drops
like some skewered starship falling to the ground.
Then there is silence all around.

When darkness descends like a safety curtain,
nature puts mourning on –
only the cross seems lit from within.
I turn away into the room
and Ponty gets up and stands behind me,
feeling for my waist like a blind man
who somehow knows it's dark for everyone.

The questions that neither of us can answer:
why did Jesus submit to all this?
When things started to get dangerous for him,
why did he not retire to a small cottage
by the Sea of Galilee?
What led him to this place?
In all the earth and the heavens,
what enabled him to endure?

Cross

Questions for reflection

1. The questions that haunt Pontius Pilate and his wife trouble many people: *What led Jesus to this place? What enabled him to endure?* How would you answer these questions for yourself?

2. The passion story has a variety of different characters and responses to Jesus: the chief priests, the accusers, the soldiers, the women of Galilee, the disciples (especially Judas and Peter), the two thieves, and so on. There is a whole gallery of contrasting people, reacting to what is happening to Jesus in different ways. In the passion story, who would you be standing beside? Where do you think you would fit in?

3. "Greater love has no one than this, that a man lay down his life for his friends." Who, if anyone, would *you* be willing to die for? For what cause, if any, would you gladly lay down your life? What could happen in your life that might make your own survival a secondary issue?

4. Much of life is untidy, ambiguous and unclear. Not every situation has an easy exit or a neat solution. Sometimes in life the only thing you can do is to endure, hang on, hang in there. Can you think of examples in your own life when you decided that the right option for you, at that time, was to brave the torment and endure?

5. Many people suffer in the cause of right, for the sake of justice, or for the sake of love. They can see a clear point to their suffering. The French philosopher Jacques Maritain said: "It is a lucky man who knows why he suffers." So much suffering in life seems meaningless when you see no purpose in it; it all seems so pointless. When you reflect on your own life, how would you rate the times you have suffered: purposeful or pointless?

Final prayer and blessing

We pray for all who suffer
in the cause of right,
for those who give their lives for a purpose
larger than their own safety and survival.
That their generosity of spirit
might meet its own reward
in the fullness of everlasting life.

We pray for those who are afflicted
by an unexpected death;
for those whose lives are
cut short by accident;
for those who are killed through violence or
terror or war;
for all who die out of due season.
That the Lord of all mercies
will make good their loss in this life
and gladden them with the glory of heaven.

We pray for those who mourn the loss
of those they have loved long and well.
That their sorrow might be free from hopeless
grief and from the agony of bitter regrets.
We pray that they might mourn in hope,
knowing that the one who is
Alpha and Omega
embraces the living and the dead
in his loving compassion and purpose.

> May the Lord of the living and the dead
> give us the assurance
> of his everlasting kindness
> in good times and in bad.
> Amen.

On the road again

Station Seven

On the road again

Old experience, new meaning

Maude and Michael have been happily married for six years. It hasn't been bliss all the way, but they've become the best of friends in their struggle to live a genuine life, sharing their love with each other and their two children. One evening Michael has a meal out with an old friend, John, who was best man at his wedding. Michael is a defence lawyer, good enough at his job, whose passion is for his family; John is a brilliant prosecutor, whose energy is for his work. They reminisce about shared days at university and court, and as Michael begins to talk about his family life he tells John, with delight, how he has loved Maude from the first moment he set eyes on her.

John – you can see him in the picture, in the open-necked shirt – is genuinely puzzled by Michael's assertion. John has an excellent memory for detail, but he sees everything in terms of black and white, right or wrong, and is anxious to get details right. He believes that the way he sees the world equals objective truth, and he is rarely open to correction; he prides himself on his objectivity, having spent his life ridding himself of anything that might look like passion.

When John checks his formidable memory, he feels compelled to correct his friend and play prosecutor. He says: "Michael, old son, you've got it wrong – you've forgotten that I introduced you to Maude. Remember? I was there when you first met her. You heard her talking at a party in my house – I remember it clearly – and she was talking loudly and for long, and you made the passing remark to me that whoever married her would be bonded unto death to a loudspeaker with no off switch! That's how I remember it, Michael, and believe me, that's how it was."

Two memories of the same event collide: which of them is right?

John remembers the event in its clinical exactness, and reports faithfully what he heard and what he saw happen. For John, there is no other way to look at it than his way. But Michael sees things differently, in a more nuanced way, refusing to limit the significance of his first meeting with Maude to the time of its happening. Michael *recollects* the event, now interpreting it as something more – a meeting that led to where he is now. Because Michael is in love with Maude now and they share a life together, he takes that love back in time and

Journey — Wilderness · Well · Mountain · Road · Table · Cross · Road

memory refers to the past and hope to the future, we – like Michael – remember and hope *from where we are now*. Depending on our present condition and mood, so we remember and so we hope. How we remember and how we hope reflect what condition we're in now.

Because of new insight and new experiences, the past can be reinterpreted and understood anew. So, too, can the way we look at the future.

The past is not dead; it waits patiently to be recollected and reinterpreted. Because we change, we review our past differently. We keep reinterpreting the past in the light of what is going on now in our lives. What appeared to be a mountain at the time turns out, later, to be a molehill; what appeared to be a chance encounter, way back then, becomes the most important meeting of our lives. Often the meaning of an experience is unclear at the time of the experience. We have to wait for meaning. Only then can we understand.

The difference is noted in everyday language: instinctively we know there is a difference between what actually happens (the event) and what is going on (the

invests the past with a new significance. His relationship with Maude affects the way he remembers their beginnings: he gives their first meeting a significance it never had at the time because he now reads it in the light of his present love. The power of his passionate love actually changes the way he reads the past. On the other hand, John's focus on exact detail means he's missed the bigger picture.

All of us bring time to mind through our awareness of the present, our memory of the past and our hope in the future. We can also choose to ignore the present, forget the past and despair about the future. Although

meaning). If a teacher sees two boys fighting outside her window, she might go outside and demand to know: "What is going on here?" She knows what is happening – they're fighting – but the question is why.

Jesus made the distinction between seeing and hearing on one hand, and perceiving and understanding on the other. You can see that difference outlined in the following table:

What actually happens	What is going on
the experience the fact the event "You shall see and hear"	the meaning the interpretation the significance "But you shall not perceive or understand"

It does not follow that because we see and hear, we thereby get the message. Maybe, as T.S. Eliot noted, "We had the experience but missed the meaning."[1] More often than not, the meaning of an experience is not given at the time of the experience; the significance of an event is not available at the time of its happening. Some experiences have to wait; the "whole story" can never be told until the experience and the meaning are put together.

Making sense of Jesus' death

In Luke's beautiful story of the road to Emmaus, you see how the two disciples are struggling to make sense of a recent event: the death of Jesus. They leave Jerusalem over their shoulder as the place where their hopes met with final defeat. When a stranger joins them on the road, they tell the story of their disappointment. Jesus, the one they had hoped would set Israel free, is now dead. In their story it becomes clear that they cannot hold the two things together: their hope in Jesus and his death. The death of Jesus cancels out their hope. Thus they feel hopeless and helpless.

The two disciples cannot understand how the death of Jesus can be understood as anything more than a tragic end to a life of promise. Like most people they believe that if you haven't achieved what you set out to do before your death, you will never achieve it in death itself. When you are dead, it's too late for everything. Death is the end of the road of promise. So the disciples mourn not only the death of Jesus but the death of their relationship with him. Now they are ex-disciples of a dead prophet. With faces to match their story.

Only when they have finished their own story does the stranger begin his own. He invites them to look at the past again, this time in a larger context, in the light of scripture. He gives a wholly different interpretation of the same event: the death of Christ was essential for his glory. According to the stranger, the death of Jesus was the achievement of his mission – not the collapse of it.

As the stranger helps the two disciples to make sense of the past in a new light, they respond by inviting him to stay with them. When they go in to table they break bread together. The stranger gives himself away by giving himself away to them. He is the risen Jesus, and he leaves them with hearts that burn and with eyes that see. Not only does he help them to interpret the past in their new experience of him as Lord, he gives them a new future. They can now face Jerusalem even in the dark, and they return there to share their story with the others.

Bringing the past up to date
In their new experience of Jesus as Lord, the disciples' past is changed. They can now revisit the past with the new light and the new love that they have experienced. They take the light of Easter Sunday back into the darkness of Good Friday, and everything looks different now. Only the risen Jesus makes sense of everything that went before. In his word and in the breaking of the bread the past is brought up to date. The past is now interpreted in the light of the great truth that Jesus is risen and is Lord.

[1] T.S. Eliot, "The Dry Salvages", *Four Quartets* (London: Faber & Faber, 2001).

Road

Gospel text: Luke 24:13-35

Now on that same day two of them were going to a village called Emmaus, about seven miles from Jerusalem, and talking with each other about all these things that had happened. While they were talking and discussing, Jesus himself came near and went with them, but their eyes were kept from recognizing him. And he said to them, "What are you discussing with each other while you walk along?" They stood still, looking sad.

Then one of them, whose name was Cleopas, answered him, "Are you the only stranger in Jerusalem who does not know the things that have taken place there in these days?" He asked them, "What things?" They replied, "The things about Jesus of Nazareth, who was a prophet mighty in deed and word before God and all the people, and how our chief priests and leaders handed him over to be condemned to death and crucified him. But we had hoped that he was the one to redeem Israel. Yes, and besides all this, it is now the third day since these things took place. Moreover, some women of our group astounded us. They were at the tomb early this morning, and when they did not find his body there, they came back and told us that they had indeed seen a vision of angels who said that he was alive. Some of those who were with us went to the tomb and found it

just as the women had said; but they did not see him." Then he said to them, "Oh, how foolish you are, and how slow of heart to believe all that the prophets have declared! Was it not necessary that the Messiah should suffer these things and then enter into his glory?" Then beginning with Moses and all the prophets, he interpreted to them the things about himself in all the scriptures.

As they came near the village to which they were going, he walked ahead as if he were going on. But they urged him strongly, saying, "Stay with us, because it is almost evening and the day is now nearly over." So he went in to stay with them. When he was at the table with them, he took bread, blessed and broke it, and gave it to them. Then their eyes were opened, and they recognized him; and he vanished from their sight. They said to each other, "Were not our hearts burning within us while he was talking to us on the road, while he was opening the scriptures to us?" That same hour they got up and returned to Jerusalem; and they found the eleven and their companions gathered together. They were saying, "The Lord has risen indeed, and he has appeared to Simon!" Then they told what had happened on the road, and how he had been made known to them in the breaking of the bread.

Journey Wilderness Well Mountain Road Table Cross Road

Road

Reflecting on the Gospel story

The story of Emmaus is unique in the New Testament because it is the only narrative that allows us to listen to how disciples of Jesus interpret his death immediately following the event. We meet two disciples heading away from Jerusalem, the place that is identified as the graveyard of their hopes. Although we cannot identify the village of Emmaus, it is the road that is important, one of the famous lost roads of history. With such a catastrophic loss behind them, it seems likely that the two disciples are heading home to Galilee, where, no doubt, they will try to pick up the old rhythm of the lives they led before they met Jesus.

One of the disciples is identified as Cleopas. The evangelist John identifies one of the Marys at the foot of the cross as Mary the wife of Clopas, or Cleopas (John 19:25). This might suggest that Cleopas' companion on this road is not another male disciple, but his wife Mary. Whatever the identities of the two disciples, the narrative focuses on their condition as two people who are overcome by their own loss, frankly bewildered by the violent turn of recent events. They speak out of their experience of Jesus: that he proved himself a prophet mighty in deed and word in the

sight of God and the people. They go on to speak of their expectation of Jesus: they had hopes that he would be the one to set Israel free.

We listen to Cleopas as he puts together both the disciples' *experience* of Jesus and their *expectations* of him. This association makes sense, since we not only have experience of people, but our positive experience of others leads us to have expectations of them. If having experience of people means that we learn about them over time, our expectations of them are deepened the more positive our experience is; our expectations are nourished by respect and familiarity, because we are given additional ground to hope through what we see in their behaviour.

Cleopas shares the sad news that he and his companion's expectations about Jesus are now well and truly ended: "But we had hoped that he was the one to redeem Israel" (Luke 24:21). Their hopes are in the past-perfect tense: it is not only the body of Jesus that has been buried; their hope in Jesus has been buried as well. Who they were was tied to who they believed he was; they were disciples because he was their master and teacher. Their governing

self-identity as disciples of Jesus has been shattered; they are identified by what they were, now literally "has-beens".

Experience means learning through direct personal contact with people and things, and new experiences or new information can challenge people to think again. The disciples are forced by their *new* experience of the death of Jesus not only to reassess Jesus but also to reassess themselves. Now they are former disciples of a dead prophet with nowhere to go but away from Jerusalem, the place where everything went wrong. And, by any account, that is not a great self-identity to be carrying on any road.

The phrase, "Oh, we had great hopes for him", is one that we hear at the funerals of those who have died out of season. Parents, relatives and friends share the sad recognition that an untimely death also means that they have to give up any hopes they cherished for the dead person. Death and hope are not good conversation partners.

Cleopas explains the reason for abandoning hope in Jesus: "our chief priests and leaders handed him over to be condemned

to death and crucified him" (24:20). Jesus did not die of old age or natural causes or by accident: his death was an execution organised by the hierarchy and effected by the civil authority. It was not done secretly at night but in public at high noon, in full view of everyone; what happened did not take place in a corner (Acts 26:26). In fact it was so public that Cleopas earlier wondered about his fellow traveller: "Are you the only stranger in Jerusalem who does not know the things that have taken place there in these days?" (Luke 24:18). The death sentence, authorised and executed by the highest authorities, seems to proclaim with finality the official legal estimation of Jesus as a criminal, the one the disciples knew as the prophet mighty in deed and word. Two contrary estimates collide: the official one seems to be the decisive one.

Experience and expectation

The disciples look on the death of Jesus, as many probably did, as the end of a promising calling, not the fulfilment of a promised one. Their hope that Jesus would prove to be the awaited Messiah is now cancelled by their experience of what has happened to him. In that sense, one has to acknowledge the disciples' level-headedness: they do not hold fast to their hopes when their experience tells them otherwise. Their expectations have been reluctantly laid down in the tomb, beside the dead body of Jesus.

Our expectations are always modified in the light of our experience. If expectations about others or situations mostly grow out of our experience, our experience tends to have the final say. If we know that someone is dead, why would we bother placing our hope in him or her? Expectations are deepened, modified or cancelled in the light of what we learn over time. Only fools or saints hold fast to their hopes when hard reality tells them the ground of their hope has collapsed. I say "saints" because there is another perspective.

Václav Havel, former president of the Czech Republic and a political prisoner for years, was asked in an interview: "Do you see a grain of hope anywhere?" He replied:

"I should probably say first that the kind of hope I often think about (especially in situations that are particularly hopeless, such as prison) I understand above all as a state of mind, not a state of the world. Either we have hope within us or we don't; it is a dimension of the soul, and it's not essentially dependent on some particular observation of the world or estimate of the situation. Hope is not prognostication. It is an orientation of the spirit, an orientation of the heart; it transcends the world that is immediately experienced, and is anchored somewhere beyond its horizons.

I think the deepest and most important form of hope, the only one that can keep us above the water, and the only true source of the breathtaking dimension of the human spirit and its efforts, is something we get, as it were, from 'elsewhere'."[2]

That observation is a profound one: hope is "not essentially dependent on some particular observation of the world or estimate of the situation". Hope is not prognostication; prognosis means literally

"to know before", like a doctor who forecasts a patient's future in the light of the symptoms the doctor sees. Prognostication is based on the evidence; hope comes from elsewhere.

The disciples are stuck in the present as a place they see as profoundly hopeless. They have been abandoned by Jesus in death; he has been violently taken from them. Since they have no "elsewhere" from which to fund their injured hope, it dies. All the signs they see point unambiguously to the double truth that not only is Jesus finished but so too is their own discipleship.

Their situation parallels a growing number of people in the Church today and many who have left the Church over their shoulders, as the disciples did Jerusalem. A considerable number of people leave the Church not because of an argument with a priest or as a protest against official church teaching, but because what was once alive now seems dead, what was once appealing now seems wearisome. For many, the sacramental life of the Church has ceased to matter in a world of competing interests. As one mother said to me: "I ended up following the example of my children by lapsing. At first I felt guilty, but the guilt soon evaporated and I was surprised to discover that I wasn't really missing anything at all."

Some wonder if there will be a future for the Christian community in Western Europe, one that is in concert with its past, or whether it will gradually but surely diminish to the level of a small community. People look around them and hunt the horizon for signs of new hope.

There is a sense in which we can see the two disciples on the road to Emmaus as our contemporaries, fellow travellers journeying through a grey landscape of ambiguity and disappointment, where, in the uncertain light of what is seen and sensed, so many cherished hopes, now withered, have been relegated to lost causes. Yet the story of their loss is what we call Gospel, what we name as scripture. When their story is proclaimed in the assembly, the priest adds the words, "This is the Gospel of the Lord." What the disciples saw as hopeless we interpret as good news, not least because we interpret their story in the larger frame of scripture. And that is what the risen Jesus does in response to his two disciples.

[2] V. Havel, *Disturbing the Peace* (New York: Vintage, 1991), p. 181.

Looking at the present as a place of hope
Towards evening, the risen Jesus, still a stranger, reinterprets his disciples' experience of recent events in the light of the past story contained in scripture. He offers a different interpretation of the same events the disciples have described, one that tries to make sense of pain and rejection and brokenness. In this section of the narrative Luke employs a strategy that is not peculiar to theological interpretations but is used in other disciplines, for instance in psychiatry and therapeutic counselling. Often when a client goes for counselling, what prompts the need is some sense of having lost one's way or feeling powerless when it comes to coping with everyday living and its demands or being unable to make any sense of what is happening in one's life.

While the client's conversation starts with describing the current crisis, the counsellor always tries to get a sense of the bigger picture. Who we are today is not explained by today but by the sum of our yesterdays. The key to unravelling the present lies somewhere in the past; the answer to why we are the way we are today is concealed in what has already happened. The dynamic is to stop staring at the present moment, the place of pain, and travel backwards into the old story in the hope that, seeing the new event in this larger context, one can understand not only what is happening but also what is going on. Thus associations with events in the past are sought to make sense of what is happening now.

In the narrative we watch Jesus moving away from an exclusive inspection of the details of what has happened during "these last few days" to placing that story into the context of prophecy. This is always done in the belief that this larger context can help to understand the immediate frame of the new event. In this, as he does elsewhere, Luke is not just reflecting on what has happened, but presenting his interpretation in the perspective of faith and prophecy. It is this perspective that will be the source of new insight. The circle of association, beginning with the new experience/event, reaches back in time to ancient stories, and returns to reinterpret the new experience in the light of that journey of discernment.

In the case of Luke's interpretation there is a double dynamic: it is not only the present that is reinterpreted in the light of the past; the past is also re-evaluated in the light of recent events. In a sense

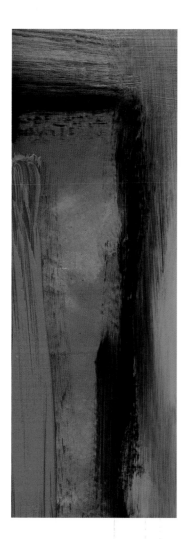

the past is rewritten to catch up with new revelation. Thus, for example, nowhere in the Old Testament or in any writings of pre-Christian Judaism is it written that the Christ *must* suffer. While Luke does not specify any passages to support his reading of scripture, he recasts the ancient understanding of the Messiah to catch up with recent events in the story of Jesus, the one who is now recognised as "Lord and Messiah" (Acts 2:36). Luke construes the suffering of Jesus as a necessary preface to glory, the splendour associated with the Messiah.

The practice of assessing the past afresh in the light of new events is something we do ourselves periodically, and sometimes we discover how time dramatically alters our perception of events. We can probably think of an event in our own past that *at the time it happened* did not register as critical or significant in our life story; only when we look back at our life from a different vantage point do we appreciate how important that event was for the course of our life.

More often than not, the significance of an experience or an event is not offered at the time it happens; sometimes we have to wait months or even years before we can truly appreciate the importance that some events have exercised in our life story. The past is not dead; it lingers on as a resource for meaning or it waits for new interpretation. If life happens chronologically, its meaning does not come to us in such a linear fashion – which is why the American playwright Arthur Miller entitled his insightful biography *Timebends*.[3]

The teaching exercise of opening up of scripture is not an academic one, but one that is eminently practical: its purpose is to reinterpret the experience of the two disciples in such a way that a sense of divine providence is intelligible in what has happened these last few days. If St Jerome's ancient maxim holds true – "Ignorance of scripture is ignorance of Christ" – then the disciples are ignorant of their own sacred tradition, and that unawareness deprives them of making sense of their own experience. Even so, the new perceptiveness does not lead the disciples to recognise the identity of their fellow traveller.

Luke manages the story with a shrewd use of suspense: while the revelation on the road leads to burning hearts, the

[3] A. Miller, *Timebends: A Life* (London: Methuen, 1987).

recognition itself is reserved for table fellowship. I would imagine another factor at play here, namely that Luke is writing for a community who will never meet the risen Lord on whatever roads they travel, but have an opportunity to meet him in the breaking of the bread. As Michael Goulder wryly observes: "But of course Christ's being known in the breaking of the bread, and his immediate vanishing, are a part of the weekly experience of every Christian at the Eucharist."[4]

The structure of the Emmaus story, at the heart of which is the breaking of the bread, gives the Christian community a perfect reminder of coming to know Jesus as Lord in the Eucharist:

> - the coming together
> - the hearing of the story
> - the gathering around the table
> - the breaking of the bread
> - the recognition of Jesus as Lord
> - the renewal of personal discipleship
> - the departure to share the new experience as good news.

In the light of their *new* experience, their recognition of the risen Jesus, the disciples again reassess their past: a recent past of injured hope is now healed in this fresh revelation. They are now able to understand why their hearts were burning within them. Their new experience enables them to make sense not only of the last few days but also of why they felt the way they did on the road when the stranger was unfolding scripture to them. The recent and the immediate past are again reappraised in the light of new awareness and insight; they are liberated from their own tragic interpretation of the last days of Jesus and their own self-image as leftover disciples of a dead prophet.

Their new experience gives them a new sense of purpose and a new authority, so they go back to the place they longed to leave over their shoulder. Jerusalem is now their chosen destination, not the city they discarded earlier in the day. Even though the day is far spent, they go back; their return is not only to a place but, more importantly, to rejoin a community, one they presumably believe to be as wretched and desolate as they were at the beginning of their journey. When they return, they share their experience of what happened to them on the road and at table.

That experience marks the beginning of their new lives.

Summary

Luke's story of the two disciples of Emmaus is heard by many people as a contemporary reflection of their experience. Two disciples openly share their disappointment and loss on the road; they do not disguise how they see things; they tell the story of how they lost their dreams and their hopes. They are joined by Jesus, who listens to them and opens their minds to a larger perspective than their limited experience. In going to table, the disciples meet the one they thought had gone for ever, in the breaking of the bread. That experience enlivens them to take the road back to Jerusalem and share their new experience with their companions.

Prayer

Batter my heart, three-personed God, for you
As yet but knock, breathe, shine, and seek to mend;
That I may rise and stand, o'erthrow me and bend
Your force to break, blow, burn, and make me new...

Yet dearly I love you and would be loved fain,
But am betrothed unto your enemy.
Divorce me, untie, or break that knot again,
Take me to you, imprison me, for I,
Except you enthral me, never shall be free,
Nor ever chaste except you ravish me.

John Donne

4 M. Goulder, *Luke: A New Paradigm*, Vol II (Sheffield: JSOT Press, 1989), p.83.

Mary, the wife of Cleopas

Everyone seems to be leaving Jerusalem. The city is emptying as if there's been news of a coming earthquake, but it's only the end of another festival. Passover is over for another year. The gates of the city are crowded with the press of people eager to get back to whatever they left behind them.

Whether my husband Cleopas or I will ever get back to ordinary life again is doubtful. Passover, for us, has been a deadly affair, a time of unutterable misery. Everything that could go wrong has gone wrong. Our beloved master, Jesus of Nazareth, is dead. And he didn't die peacefully in his bed, but he was put to death, in the cruellest fashion, by the authorities we have been educated to respect.

As the two of us take the road to Emmaus, we are heart-sore from grief, from the senselessness of it all. Looking at Cleopas I think my heart will break: he looks like a man who has lost everything in life but the breath in his body. It's as if his loss has scaled away everything I've known of him, stripped him of his appetite for life and his easy good humour, revealing not the man I know and love but a disconsolate angel with nothing to say and nowhere to go but away from a once-heavenly city.

He has no tears left in him.

The road we're taking to Emmaus, which winds through Gabaon and Beth-horon, is quiet. We have left the crush of pilgrims behind us, most of whom will be heading north. It is hot. Even the sun seems to miss nothing under its merciless clarity, blistering everything around us. The geography is comfortless. We live in a land of too much light, too many rocks, too much zeal. There is no shade or shadow or nuance. Or is this just my hurt talking?

Is it any wonder I loved Jesus so much? His very difference made him religious. He spoke to us of God through living water, wheat fields, vineyards, fruit trees, flowers, fish, bread and wine. He greened our landscape with virtue; he humanised it with stories of ordinary people. His victories were of love, trust, forgiveness, tenderness, forbearance. If you're a woman you get a wee bit tired listening to talk about the glory of the battlefield and the majesty of the mountain, as if these are the only places you can meet God. You want God in the kitchen, in the miracle of daily bread, in the majesty of everyday love, in the grandeur of your sleeping child's face. Jesus gave us all this. Little wonder he said his kingdom was not of this world.

But Jesus is dead now. And the best in us has died with him.

"What will become of us now?" I ask Cleopas. Up to now he has said nothing, probably because he thinks there is nothing to say; but I just want to hear him speak, say something, anything. He draws in a breath, hunches his shoulders, and breathes out loudly as if trying to expel some of the hopelessness within. I can see the sweat on his forehead and above his upper lip.

"Cleopas?"

"I heard you, Mary," he says. "I heard you." His voice seems to come to me from a great distance. "I wish there was something I could say to cheer you."

I'm thinking of something to say to Cleopas, for I'm afraid we might lapse into another long silence, when I become aware of someone close behind us. When I turn my head to look, I see a man striding towards us, his head uncovered, his long arms swinging by his side. He looks like a man in a hurry to be somewhere, someone who has to make up for lost time; but when he gets level with us, he slows down and falls into step beside us.

"Shalom," he says, nodding to each of us in turn.

"Shalom," we murmur back.

Cleopas eyes the stranger closely and then glances over at me. I can read his tired look: what have we done to deserve this? We don't want to be rude to the stranger, but neither of us is in the mood for polite diversions. Then, as if we've previously agreed what to do in awkward moments like this, we both slacken our pace to a dawdle, to allow our unwanted travelling companion to move on and leave us in peace. But he slows down, too, and keeps walking by our side.

"What are you discussing as you walk along?" the stranger asks amiably, as if we've been discussing the weather. At the question, we are reduced to a standstill. I look at Cleopas, whose downcast face must match my own. For a long moment I think he might ignore the question, excuse us and walk on.

Cleopas clears his throat. He has his own question for the stranger: "Are you the only visitor to Jerusalem who doesn't know the things that have been happening there these last few days?"

"What things?" the stranger asks.

This new question prompts Cleopas to start walking again. This is like a bad dream, I think. How can this man be so ignorant of the trial and execution of Jesus? After all, what happened to Jesus wasn't exactly a secret affair. Or is this man one of nature's dangerous innocents, the kind of person who blithely goes through life, untouched by the offence of other people's suffering?

Looking at him, I feel my questions are unfair. What would Jesus do, I ask myself, if he were faced with this inquisitive man?

"It's difficult to know where to start," I say to him. "We are followers of Jesus of Nazareth."

"Were," corrects Cleopas.

"He's dead," I say, abruptly. "You must have heard about Jesus?"

The stranger nods his head, but I sense he is not going to speak. This question master who stole up on us so quietly seems in no rush to ask any more questions. His face is polite, withholding.

"Then it all came to an end," Cleopas says, aggrieved and suddenly alert. "And us with it. I find it difficult enough to understand why so many people turned against Jesus but I'll never be able to make out why our chief priests and leaders rejected him so finally and with such violence."

He hesitates, less sure of himself, and wipes the sweat from his forehead with the sleeve of his tunic. "Forgive me, I'm confused," he goes on. "I don't mean to question the ways

of the Almighty, but if God can send an angel to save Isaac from being slaughtered, why couldn't he do the same for Jesus? Why didn't the angel come?"

Cleopas asks the last question with such passion that it sounds like a cry for help. He looks up at the dazzling blue sky as if he might find some answer scribbled there, or might yet be surprised by some tardy angel come to undo the mistake of suffering. Whatever he is looking for, there are no answers forthcoming either from me or the reticent stranger.

For a little while we journey on in silence, left to listen to our own thoughts and the rhythm of our steps. Ahead of us the road unscrolls its way to a shifting but unvaried horizon of hills and stones and dust. I wonder if we'll ever get to the end of it. A few trees, mostly acacia or jujube, do their best to soften the harsh landscape, but their bravado seems to highlight a larger loss. Above us the sun is as it always is, vast and overriding and relentless.

This road, this heat, this journey, this stranger, this silence: is it only a matter of time, I wonder, before everything in life becomes a question?

"We had a hope," I find myself saying to the stranger. "Not just Cleopas and I, but the whole crowd of us who followed Jesus. We all hoped that he would be the one to set Israel free. We could see he was a prophet, as I said, a great prophet like Moses, but the important thing is that what we saw led us to expect more. Cleopas was always saying, 'Mark my words, Jesus is more than meets the eye.'"

"Sure I was," Cleopas says. "And I meant it at the time."

"Of course, you did," I say. I turn to our companion again. "I don't know if you know what I mean, but Jesus was the kind of person who attracted your hope. Somehow – I don't know how – our hope seemed secure with him, well placed, like a sure bet. Everything he did and said seemed to confirm that. He became everything we hoped for and more. When we looked at him we saw our hope fulfilled."

"And that's the problem," Cleopas protests, his voice unnaturally loud, his hands held out in front of him as if they hold the weight of what he's saying. "That's the sadness of it all. We burdened Jesus with too much hope. We forgot that our grand expectations could be brought down by so many other things in life."

His voice quietens and he returns his hands to his sides. He says, "Sometimes, without knowing it, you let your hope run too far ahead of you, as if hope can manage by itself in the real world. You hope that everything you cherish will endure, that time will secure what your heart yearns for, that people's evil designs will never destroy your belief in human goodness, that God will not abandon what his love has created. And then it all proves too much when your hope becomes a fatal casualty of what actually happens. That's our story. Our hope ended up being hammered to death on the cross. How can we hang on to our hope in Jesus as the Messiah when he is well and truly dead? Our hope in him can never be reclaimed, for death finishes everything, empty tomb or no empty tomb."

I don't know about the stranger, but I don't understand everything Cleopas says; I do, however, more than I can say, feel his pain and disappointment. Then, as if he can no longer contain himself, the stranger exclaims, "How foolish you are! So slow of heart to believe in all the prophets have said! Was it not necessary that the Christ should suffer all this before entering his glory?"

Cleopas and I are so stunned by the stranger's inexplicable outburst that we stop in our tracks. I see Cleopas open his mouth to say something, but only a guttural sound emerges, and, with his mouth still hanging open, he stares at the stranger as if this man has just shared some disreputable secret.

"About suffering and rejection," he continues, "the prophets were always right: look at how they lived, listen to all they said, remember how they died. The mighty prophet like Moses, the Messiah, could not have avoided the traditional destiny of the prophets if God's plan was to be accomplished. The very thing you say destroyed your hope is what makes for the fulfilment of scripture.

"You believed in a Messiah who could only succeed in his mission by detachment and power and success, never by making himself vulnerable, never by permitting himself to be wounded, never by allowing others to do to him what others do to so many innocents. You burdened yourselves with the wrong hopes.

"Believe me when I tell you that the way of the Messiah is the way of Jesus, the way of long-suffering love. Loving God is not a defence against disappointment, neither is it a guarantee of safety. Long-suffering love makes its way with a cross on its back. It takes on its shoulders what so many people are anxious to avoid: responsibility for their hate, their meanness of spirit, their violence, their legion of sins.

"You speak of the passion of Jesus as if it were only something done to Jesus. It was his own inner passion for God and for people that enabled him to make the journey from Gethsemane to Golgotha. Better for the Messiah to pass lovingly into the realm of death, for the sake of others, than dwindle into a passionless glory that costs nothing and, therefore, means nothing."

As we journey closer to Emmaus, the sun now battles with dark clouds, and the teacher does something for Cleopas and me that we could not do for ourselves: he illuminates our own experience of recent events by his deep knowledge of the word of God. Through everything he says he invites us to think again, to look again, to understand anew.

When we come to the turn-off for our village, Cleopas and I naturally turn right into the little track that leads to Emmaus, but the teacher pauses and stays on the road. Without a wave or a word of goodbye, he makes to continue his journey on the way that leads to the Great Sea.

When I see him begin to move away from us, I feel an enormous sadness come over me. It's as though I am watching yet another sign of hope withdraw from us and, without excuse or apology, head elsewhere until it becomes absorbed in some amorphous world, leaving Cleopas and me to return to our makeshift lives.

"Teacher!" Cleopas calls.

The teacher stops and turns around. Cleopas takes my hand and we both walk over to the man we don't want to lose.
"Don't go. Please," Cleopas pleads. "We would like you to stay with us. It is evening and the day is almost over."

"Come home with us," I say. "Please come home with us."

"You would honour our house," Cleopas adds rather shyly, his hand gripping mine more tightly.

Our fellow traveller smiles at us. Looking at him I get the impression he is relieved we have shortened his road. Though I cannot be certain, I think he was hoping we would ask him home. This thought delights me.

"I'll be happy to stay with you," he says.

Cleopas releases his grip on my hand and says to our guest, "Good. Let's go."

For the short time it takes to reach the village, the three of us pick our way down the stony track. Cleopas leads the way; I follow behind him; the teacher brings up the rear. None of us speaks, but I feel the silence is a happy one, expressing a new intimacy.

As the last part of the track curves sharply to the right before entering the village, our three shadows merge into one long indeterminate shape on the ground, making it look like a gawky giant hurrying to keep some rendezvous in Emmaus. I am still smiling at the thought when we reach the door of the house.

Once inside, the house seems mercifully cool compared to the heat we have endured, and the partial darkness is a welcome relief from the brightness outside. Cleopas waits inside the threshold and formally welcomes the teacher into the house by kissing him on the hand and pouring a little oil on his head. Thus anointed, the teacher is invited to sit on the low bench beside the door. As I set the table with barley bread, olives, fruit, cups and a jug of wine, Cleopas pours water into a dish and goes down on his knees to wash the feet of our guest.

I know that Cleopas, like me, must be wondering whose feet he is washing; but our tradition of courtesy forbids us to ask the name of our guest. It will be for him, if he chooses, to tell us in his own time who he is. After washing our hands, we take our place at table. Before Cleopas says a word, the teacher takes the bread and says the blessing; then he breaks the bread and hands it to Cleopas and me.

As we take the bread from our mysterious table companion, at this moment appointed by God, our eyes are opened for the first time and we behold the true identity of the stranger. It is Jesus himself, our beloved master! Cleopas and I look on the radiant face of our risen Lord, the face we believed was lost to us for ever, and we are speechless for joy, but no sooner have

we recognised him than he vanishes from sight. Suddenly, without warning, there is no one there. Suddenly there are only two of us in the room.

We both rise slowly to our feet and stare at the empty place. Never before have I looked at the shape of an absence; never before have I been so intensely aware of someone's presence. Instinctively I move over to where the Lord sat and I touch the small wooden bench, but I feel only the rough texture of the wood; I touch the table where he leaned, but it is only a table.

"He is not here, he is risen," Cleopas says softly.

"Yes," I say, now patting the air like a blind woman confused that she can't touch what she feels is there.

"Mary," Cleopas says.

I start fingering the bread Jesus held out to us. The stranger gave himself away in the breaking of this bread, I tell myself.

"Mary," Cleopas says again.

I let go of the bread, Cleopas and I turn to one another and, without a word, we fall into each other's arms and we hold one another tenderly and for a long time, until our tears stop flowing and our trembling bodies come to rest.

"Oh Mary," Cleopas says, "wasn't your heart burning within you as he talked to us on the road and explained the scriptures to us?"

"It still is," I say. "He lit a fire in our hearts and I hope it will never go out again."

"But we must go," Cleopas says, easing himself out of our embrace.

"Where?"

"To Jerusalem," he says.

"When?"

"Now, of course! We must tell the others the good news."

"Of course!" I exclaim.

Without a backward glance, we leave behind the table set for eating, the half-dark of the room, the shelter of our home; we leave behind our tiredness and sorrow and ignorance, and we retrace our steps up the track to the road, where we turn left for Jerusalem.

The sun is setting now and it casts a soft pink light over the landscape as far as the eye can see. The few acacia trees are silhouetted against a glorious sky. A short distance away, on the slopes of the hills, a vast herd of sheep is grazing; and around them, patiently taking up their positions, the shepherds prepare to gather them in for the evening, to the drystone-wall enclosures.

From somewhere on the hillside comes the plaintive sound of a shepherd's flute, the notes rising and falling in some secret signature tune to the flock. As Cleopas and I hurry on our way, the fading music spurs us on and on to a Jerusalem where new stories will be told, where new music will be played and where a remnant of disciples, made lonely by loss and disappointment, will be gathered into one fold by the undying love of the risen Lord.

Road

Questions for reflection

1. In an afternoon's walk Mary, the wife of Cleopas, journeys through a variety of emotions: from loss, disappointment and hopelessness to a burning heart on hearing a stranger help make sense of all that had happened recently. Have you ever had a similar experience, one in which you felt really stuck but someone helped you open your eyes to new possibility?

2. Like the disciples of Emmaus, everyone has a graveyard of hopes that they once cherished but have now been buried. What have you buried in your graveyard of hopes?

3. Have you ever met a stranger on your travels who really helped you?

4. The past is a source of wisdom: somewhere in our past there lies the key to understanding why we have ended up the way we are today. How often do you consult the past of your story for understanding?

5. At the end of the meal, the two disciples return to Jerusalem to share their positive experience with others. At the end of every Eucharist the priest sends the people out, to continue their journey and share something of what they have celebrated. How good are you at sharing the goodness you have received?

Journey Wilderness Well Mountain Road Table Cross Road

Final prayer and blessing

We pray for all those
who walk a road of loss and disappointment,
particularly those who have to face
the large absence of someone dear to them
or the death of a loved one:
that the Lord might join them on the road,
assuring them that their grief will not be everlasting,
but be overtaken by the power of God's abiding love.

We pray for an increase of hope
in our broken world:
that people may see signs
beyond the immediate horizons of struggle,
of deprivation, of violence.
We pray that God will continue to raise up
peacemakers in our communities,
women and men committed to building
human sanctuaries, holy places,
where poor people are honoured,
where crushed people are sheltered,
where lost people might find a home.

We pray for our own communities.
May they be places of welcome and care,
where the sorrowing find comfort,
where the lonely find fellowship,
where the faithful find grace.
Above all,
may they be places of loving respect,
where each person is recognised and reverenced
as a child of the living God.

May the good Lord
walk with us and bear with us
in all our journeys through life.
May his presence enable us to face
whatever the future holds, whatever might await us.

May we hold fast to his reassurance
that he will attend us and abide with us,
even to the ends of the earth.
Amen.

Acknowledgements

The author and publishers are grateful for permission to reproduce extracts and pictures for the following material in this volume:

© **Emma Blackwood** for permission to reproduce five original paintings:
p.15 At the Heavens, 2007;
p.39 Lost in the Moment, 2007;
p.59 Nothing Without You, 2007;
p.85 In His Image, 2007;
p.133 Reflected Image, 2007 (see www.emmablackwood.com)

The Bridgeman Art Library, UK:
p.41 The Meeting of Jacob and Rachel (oil on canvas), Dyce, William (1806-64) / © New Walk Museum, Leicester City Museum Service, UK;
p.73 Frog Prince and the Maiden, pub.1874 (illustration), Crane, Walter (1845-1915) / Anthony Crane Collection, UK;
p.120 Jesus Washing Peter's Feet, 1876 (oil on canvas), Brown, Ford Madox (1821-93) / © Manchester Art Gallery, UK.

Des Moines Art Centre, Iowa:
p.49 © Edward Hopper, Automat, 1927.

Photo Scala, Florence:
p.111 The Last Supper, Bassano, Jacopo (1515-1592) Galleria Borghese, Rome;
p.124 Black Crucifixion, Romanesque sculpture, Church of St Maria di Castello, Genoa;
p.143 Black Crucifixion (detail).

Individuals

p.65 Jock Dalrymple – Face of Christ (11th-century stained glass, France);

p.81 Denis McBride – Gilgamesh, from the Assyrian capital Khorsabad;

p.109 © Sadao Watanabe (Japan) – The Last Supper;

p.114 Ingmar Bergman – The Seventh Seal: film still from www.timeout.com/img/29566/w513/image.jpg;

p.127 George Suyeoka – Map of Jerusalem © World Book-Childcraft International, Inc;

p.137 © Kim Yong Gil (Korea) – The Crucifixion (detail);

pp.139 © Sebastien Champion (France) – Pilate's Wife.

DC Moore Gallery, New York City:

p.151 Supper, 1963, © George Tooker, egg tempera on gesso panel; private collection.

iStockphoto

for cover and pages 8, 17, 20, 23, 25, 27, 30, 32. 35, 43, 47, 52, 54, 57, 70, 75, 87, 91, 93, 95, 97, 107, 113, 117, 131, 147, 153, 157, 161, 167.

Shutterstock

for pages 11, 37, 63, 76, 78, 83, 99, 100, 102, 105, 122, 144, 163, 169, 171.

Every effort has been made to contact copyright holders. The publishers will be pleased to make good, in future editions, any errors or omissions brought to their attention.

Journeying with Jesus for Groups

A specially edited companion for group study. Ideal for those who meet regularly as well as Lenten study groups.

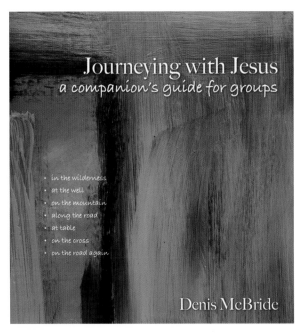

Journeying with Jesus is a deeply spiritual and lavishly resourced programme of study for those who want to journey side by side with our Lord, either individually or in small groups. We begin our journey in the wilderness, and, with Jesus, face our temptation to opt for raw power. We travel with Jesus to the top of a mountain, we walk with him along the road, we encounter a series of remarkable people Jesus attracts to himself, and finally sit with him at table before accompanying him to the cross. But the journey doesn't end there. The great joy of Easter bursts into our lives as Christ joins us again on the road. But will we recognise him?

£4.95 code: 1469
ISBN: 9780852313596
Available from Redemptorist Publications.
Please call 01420 88222 or visit our website: www.rpbooks.co.uk